A History of Weiss Lake

A History of Weiss Lake

DOUGLAS SCOTT WRIGHT

THE History PRESS

Published by The History Press
Charleston, SC 29403
www.historypress.net

Cover design by Natasha Momberger

First published 2008
Second printing 2008
Third printing 2011

Manufactured in the United States

ISBN 978.1.59629.560.5

Library of Congress Cataloging-in-Publication Data

Wright, Scott, 1970-
A history of Weiss Lake / Scott Wright.
p. cm.
Includes bibliographical references.
ISBN 978-1-59629-560-5
1. Weiss Lake (Ala.)--History. 2. Cherokee County (Ala.)--History. I. Title.
F332.C44W75 2008
976.1'65--dc22
2008038820

Notice: The information in this book is true and complete to the best of our knowledge. It is offered without guarantee on the part of the author or The History Press. The author and The History Press disclaim all liability in connection with the use of this book.

This book is dedicated to my grandmother, Sarah Elizabeth Gossett Wright, who passed away in July 2008.

CONTENTS

INTRODUCTION

When I graduated from Cedar Bluff High School in 1988, I couldn't imagine why anyone would want to live in Cherokee County, Alabama. I'd just spent eighteen consecutive years here, so I was speaking from experience. It was rural. It was quiet. Everyone knew your name because they attended high school with your momma and daddy, or at least knew someone else who had. The nearest movie theatre was thirty minutes away. The fast-food chains hadn't yet found one of the few road maps that included the county's five small towns. There was no future for an eager advertising executive-to-be in this place, I thought.

After all those years of rural quiet, I was ready for something more exciting. So I peeled out of my parents' driveway one August morning and headed two hours west, all the way to Tuscaloosa. The college town had a population four times larger than all of Cherokee County, and that ratio didn't even take into account football Saturdays in the fall. I left home with visions of earning a degree and then taking a job in a "big city," somewhere metropolitan and noisy, where the traffic signals had three colors instead of two, shops and stores stayed open after lunch on Wednesday and the police department didn't roll up the sidewalks at 5:00 p.m.

Be careful what you wish for. I've lived and worked in Tuscaloosa, Birmingham and Chattanooga, Tennessee, since graduating from the University of Alabama in 1993. To make a long story short, it took less than four years for the bustle of those big cities to hustle me back to Cherokee County. My current employer owns a T-shirt business in Centre and needed some help creating designs; a short time after he hired me in November 1996, he bought a local weekly paper, said "Here you go, Mr. Editor" and instructed me to sink or swim. Twelve years later, I'm still afloat.

Looking back on over a decade literally surrounded by Weiss Lake, I can't imagine why I ever thought I might want to tread the waters of life anywhere else. I suppose I never realized what I had here until I spent a few years cursing the clamor, dodging pedestrians and waiting for a few too many red lights to turn green. Cherokee County, Alabama, is my home, and there's no place like it. A big part of what makes this place so special, to me and the twenty-four thousand other people who live here, is Weiss (rhymes with "nice") Lake. We call it "our lake." Alabama Power may have built it, but it's ours. We like to catch the crappie and bass in it, ski across the top of it and build our homes and weekend retreats as close to the shores of it as the power company will allow—sometimes closer, even. But that's another story.

If you're a fisherman visiting for the weekend and you want to make sure everyone knows, all you have to do is mispronounce the namesake, or flip the adjective and refer to our reservoir as "Lake Weiss." The standard reply is: "Y'all must be from out of town. Welcome to Cherokee County." We mean it, too. The businesses here and the people who own and operate them rely largely on the tourism the lake generates to pay their bills and feed their families. The lake affects everyone who lives here and thousands of people all over the country who call our home theirs during holidays or for a few months in the summertime. If you visit for the weekend and bump into someone whose accent sounds a little out of place but who still insists he lives here, he's probably telling the truth. Chances are, he is a relocated fisherman from Illinois, Ohio or Indiana who finally decided he was tired of spending so much time driving to the most beautiful place in the world. Gasoline isn't getting any cheaper, after all.

For the first 125 years of its existence, Cherokee County didn't have quite so much water smack in the middle of it. There were generations of people who lived and died here knowing only the narrow, winding Coosa River and the fertile banks that composed some of the most productive farmland anywhere. Entire families lived off the land. They spent mornings, afternoons and evenings ankle-deep in the rich, brown dirt, planting and weeding and hoeing and picking. Those farmers and their wives and kids crossed the river on manually operated ferries that relied on the current of the water to travel back *and* forth, or on rickety, wooden, one-lane bridges too flimsy to support the weight of a loaded school bus. To them, the amount of water the Coosa River was already bringing into the county was plenty.

Many Cherokee County residents kept subscriptions to local and state newspapers in the 1950s solely for the purpose of following the progress of Alabama Power's efforts, for better or worse, to wash their old lifestyles away. A few foresaw the possibility that their farms and the food they needed to feed their children might soon disappear beneath a wall of water. So they organized a group of citizens and tried to fight Alabama Power's proposed permanent flood. A significant number of the county's farming families welcomed the water. They sold their land or took up other trades. A few learned to drive bulldozers, pour concrete or weld steel, and by doing so they helped transform the river that had meandered through their past into a more promising future for their children and grandchildren.

Yes sir, the city slickers we're so happy to see come driving across the county lines today had other plans for this place a half century ago. After decades of lobbying and studying and planning, Alabama Power brought in hundreds of people from Birmingham, Arkansas and dozens of other faraway places to harness the power of the Coosa and change the lives of the county's rural farmers forever. Weiss Lake will be fifty years old in 2011, and a lot has changed since the day the switch was thrown that sent the first turbine whirling, mostly for the better. Sure, there are problems. Water quality issues and the potential loss of water to fast-growing Atlanta are hot-button topics in Cherokee County as Weiss Lake nears its golden anniversary. It's funny to think that these days, the worst thought in the world to so many here is that someone might one day decide to take "our lake" away, especially considering the fight a few of the local citizenry put up to try and prevent its construction in the first place.

As far as I know, there exists no organized, comprehensive collection of the stories of the people who lived in Cherokee County before Weiss Lake was built, or of those who built it or had their lives changed by it. I hope readers will not judge too harshly if I have neglected to uncover old family tales or unique experiences that should rightfully be included—my research has made it clear that it would take a million pages to tell them all. In the months since I began this project I have felt both immensely overjoyed and, at times, horribly under qualified. I have seen grown men shed tears of happiness and sadness, and in the face of approaching deadlines, I shed a few of my own. I rekindled friendships with people I have not seen in years, and made a few new ones that I hope to be able to keep for at least the next few. I have been helped by dozens more along the way, and I am grateful to them all.

As I became involved in the process of writing this book, I realized I did not need additional reassurance that I live in the most wonderful place in the state of Alabama, and possibly all the world; my transformation from a loather to a lover of Cherokee County was complete long ago. But I am glad I dug a little deeper into the story of why and how my home came to be what it is today. This process has certainly helped me to appreciate my good fortune even more. It has also made me realize the sacrifices that will be necessary if "our lake" is to endure for another half century.

I hope people will enjoy these few stories about the history of Weiss Lake and its mostly positive effects on the people of Cherokee County. I hope my narrow view of such a massive undertaking can still somehow relate interesting insights about the reservoir's construction, its aftereffects and its future. I'd like to think people will enjoy reading these stories as much as I enjoyed gathering them together and writing them down, but that may be asking the impossible.

THE DAMMED PAST

A land without history is a land without hope.
—Hugh Cardon, quoting an anonymous historian, Coosa River News, *1936*

1540–1920

An article written in 1936 by Mr. Hugh Cardon for the now-defunct *Coosa River News* looked back on the first hundred years of Cherokee County history. Cardon was a "much respected historian of the county and collector of antique and Indian artifacts," according to a description in a book compiled by the Cherokee County Historical Museum in the early 1970s. The book, loosely bound with staples and a cardboard cover, reprinted Cardon's work in its entirety, then told the story of various communities in the county before moving on to schools, people, transportation and communication. The book even touched on the county's experiences during the Civil War and the sixty years after it ended, and it is undoubtedly among the most complete histories of the first century of Cherokee County in existence. Despite its hodgepodge of typefaces, ill-defined borders and tendency to come apart after only a few pages, *History and Heritage: Articles on Cherokee County, Alabama* tells a story that anyone who is interested in the history of Weiss Lake needs to know a little about, whether they realize it or not.

Hernando De Soto, the first white man to ever set foot in what would later become northeastern Alabama, is mentioned early and often in Cardon's text. The Spanish explorer invaded the area in 1540 with several hundred soldiers, slaves and pigs in tow and "stood on the banks of the Coosa before the great Indian city of Chiaha." De Soto came to the New World in search

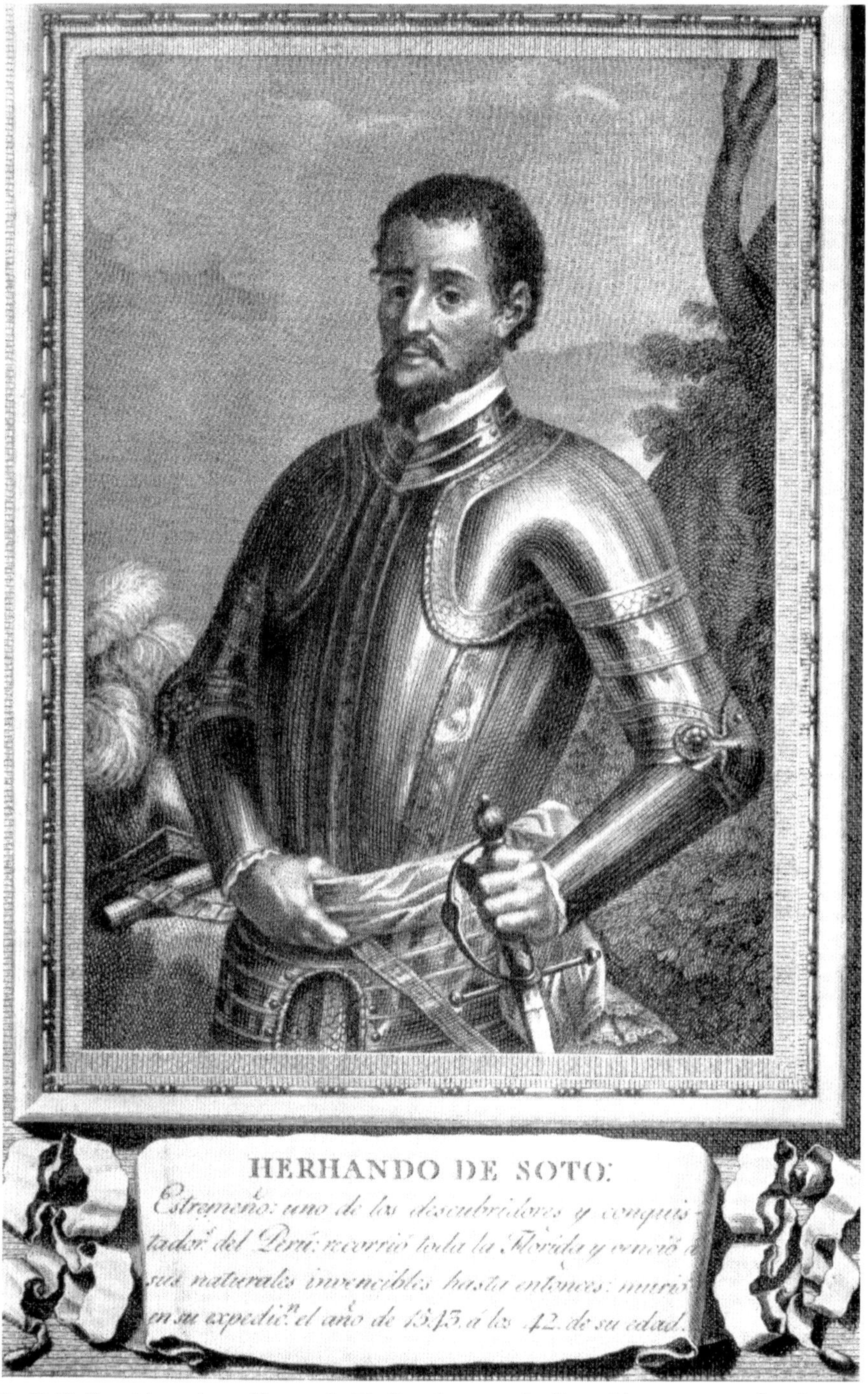

In 1540, Spanish explorer Hernando De Soto became the first white man to set foot in what eventually became Cherokee County, Alabama. *Courtesy of the National Archives.*

of gold, but all he ever found in what would eventually come to be known as Cherokee County was a tribe of Indians who only wanted to see all those white men and their smelly herd of pigs head farther downstream as quickly as possible. There is some dispute over exactly where the ancient Indian village of Chiaha was, as Cardon pointed out in his article. "Scientifically and patriotically," he wrote, "we maintain that it was located on McCoy's Island," a large clump of fertile land that once split the Coosa near Poole's Ferry. (In the interest of simplicity, and because this book is being written by a fellow Cherokee County native, Cardon's interpretation of the historical record is considered indisputable.) So it was in the area around Cedar Bluff that De Soto and his mobile stockyard spent several days and for the first time saw "the products of a soil more fertile than any their eyes had ever beheld." The Coosa River had, it seems, been supplying sustenance to the people who lived along its banks long before Alabama Power Company poured all that concrete in its way.

After De Soto left and took his scribes and journals with him, the wedge-shaped corner of the world that eventually became Cherokee County may as well have dropped off the face of the planet. As Cardon wrote, "From 1540 to 1816 we know very little of what happened within the bounds of this county, but suppose it was occupied by the Cherokee and Creek Indians." Cardon recalled the words of historian James Albert Pickett, whose 1851 book titled *History of Alabama* mentioned how clean, healthy and intelligent the Indians who lived in the area seemed to him. He also mentioned their pleasant language. "The truth of Pickett's statement will not be doubted," Cardon wrote, "when we speak aloud some of their words, such as 'Chattooga,' 'Oostanala,' and 'Coosa.'" Around 1770, those same Indians established Turkey Town, a community along an Indian trail that headed off toward Guntersville, Alabama, in one direction and Cave Spring, Georgia, in the other. It was at Turkey Town in October 1816 that the end began for the Creeks and Cherokees, when "a council was held…to settle the boundaries and ratify a peace treaty" with the United States government. Unfortunately, history is filled with reminders of how honorably the federal government behaved when it came to signed agreements with this country's original inhabitants. Twenty years later, the Creeks and Cherokees were on a forced march to Oklahoma, just in time to make room for wagonloads of East Coasters anxious to make northeast Alabama their new home.

One of the first families of settlers relocated to the area in 1835. Whitfield Anthony, a Methodist preacher, "brought with him to this county his family and several other families from Georgia and South Carolina, numbering in all about forty." According to Cardon, they settled "about three miles west of the mouth of Mud Creek" and took up farming. Forty years later, the Reverend J.D. Anthony, son of Whitfield Anthony, wrote down his boyhood recollections of his family's move to Cherokee County for a story in the *Gadsden Times*. He listed several neighbors he could recall, including "the first justice of the peace," a man who was "the father of several girls" and a man named John Lay. Coincidentally, John Lay was the grandfather of William Patrick Lay, one of the three men who later founded Alabama Power Company.

When it was created on January 9, 1836, Cherokee County was already a farming community, and the lifestyles of the people who lived in the

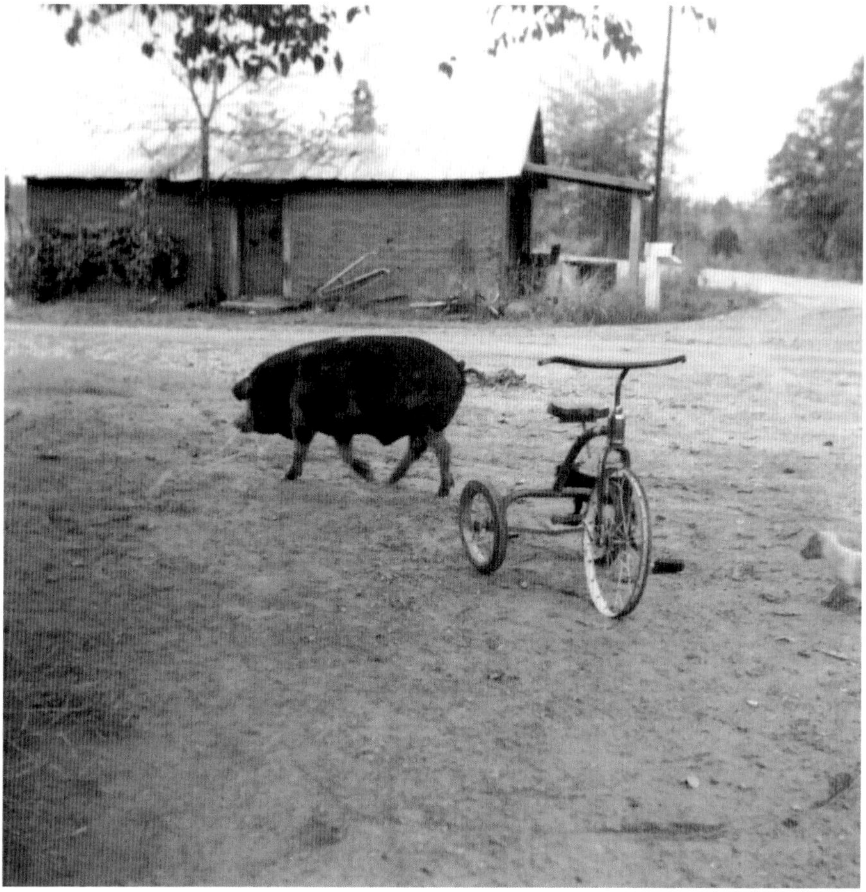

The front yard of Lewis and Sarah Wright, circa 1958, illustrates Cherokee County's rural setting in the years before Weiss Lake was built. *Courtesy of Julia Coheley.*

northeast corner of Alabama, thirty miles from Rome, Georgia, and less than ninety miles from both Atlanta and Chattanooga, Tennessee, didn't change much over the next 120 years. Men, women and children farmed, milled and then farmed some more. They milked cows in the early morning, hoed long rows or filled huge bags with cotton until dusk, then walked to the nearest creek to wash a day's worth of dirt from behind their ears and under their toenails so they could get up at dawn the next morning and start all over again—unless it was Sunday. On the Sabbath, they would spend the day dreading the night because they knew the next light they'd see would be shining in their eyes from just over the horizon as they walked to the cotton fields on Monday morning.

In his book *REA Pioneer and Lifelong Democrat*, Cherokee County resident Roscoe Young described everyday life on his father's farm in Cherokee County in the early 1900s:

> *My father grew mostly cotton, We cultivated our farm with mules. We always had from six to ten mules. We grew very little corn and hay to feed the stock but bought it over on the Tennessee River Valley. Papa owned a cotton gin. He bought cotton and cottonseed, and then he would sell it in Rome, Georgia. He also sold fertilizer to the farmers and sold coal to heat the schools in Cherokee County...We picked a few acres of strawberries, and I remember* [customers] *paying two cents a quart for picking...The clothes were washed outside the house and then batted with a paddle on a large block of wood, made out of a tree trunk, to get the dirt out.*

Sarah Elizabeth Gossett Wright, a native of Calhoun County, humorously related similar simplistic experiences about life on the farm in Cherokee County in a book of family stories titled *Recollections*, published privately in 1981:

> *We were so poor, but never hungry. We always had big gardens and canned our vegetables, and had hogs and cows, so we were about as well off as our neighbors...The Alabama Power Company finally decided to build a dam on the darn river, and bought most of our bottom land, and eventually the flood water covered most of the crawfishy land and that is as near milk and honey as I ever had in Cherokee County!*

James L. Wright, who was born in 1945, remembered the fields he and his older siblings farmed in the early 1950s. He also described the "crawfishy" land his mother was so happy to see taken by the lake:

> *I don't know how many acres we actually cultivated, but daddy lost around 250 acres in the lake. We had a corn picker that we used to bring in the corn, but we picked the cotton by hand. Then we'd sell it at Lindsey's gin. They'd buy everything. They'd buy all the cotton and corn and then sell the cottonseed to Rome Oil Mill to make cooking oil. Cherokee Milling bought people's corn, too. I remember hauling bales of hay and corn to Cherokee Milling and having them crush it up for cow feed.*

Cherokee County wasn't exclusively a farming community, just mostly. By the 1890s, the community of Pleasant Gap was "a busy center of activity," according to Bill Anthony in an article in *History and Heritage.* The community featured "several stores, a saw mill, gin, post office, flour mill and a brick factory. Several freight trains and a passenger train made daily stops." A man named Stroup built a thirty-two-foot-tall furnace near the now-flooded town of Round Mountain in 1849 that, at the height of operation, consumed 650 acres of charcoal and produced two and a half tons of iron ore every day. The community of Pope, a trading post seven miles south of Centre on the road to Piedmont, featured "a post office, a blacksmith and a large commissary." The Rock Run Iron Company was in business by the mid-1880s; Spring Garden—or Ambersonville, if you prefer the original name—doesn't even have its own postal delivery today, but a hundred years ago it was a cotton center in the county, complete with "a drug store, barber shop, saw mill and livery stable." The boomtown of Bluffton was once so big it had over eight thousand residents and plans for a university. (Today, it's not even a spot on the map.)

While towns and business centers popped up and then died out in Cherokee County, residents fought each other over the location of the county seat (the newly created town of Centre, named for its spot near the center of the county, won out over Cedar Bluff in 1844) and fought the damned Yankees in places like Shiloh and Missionary Ridge in the early 1860s. Mostly because of its place along the river, Cedar Bluff remained a valuable trading post after the courthouse moved, according to the March 29, 1901 edition of the *Coosa River News*. Reporter Robert Lawrence wrote that the town contained "six or eight merchandise establishments, three or four saloons, a wagon and buggy shop, blacksmith shop, harness shop, etc.," until a few years after the Civil War. In 1900, according to Thelma Slone in *History and Heritage*, Cedar Bluff was a thriving farm community. "In the fall of the year things were buzzing with cotton buying as Cedar Bluff was the best cotton market on the river this side of Rome. There was a boat on the river twice a week."

Cherokee County native Billy Godfrey, born in 1918, remembered being a boy of about fourteen the last time a steamboat came struggling up the Coosa River.

> *I saw that old steamboat; it came up the river one time. I was in school that day and we heard the whistle and everyone took off out the building to see that steamboat, because none of us had ever seen one before. We all got a whipping for that. They had about quit running up and down the river by around 1912, something like that. They were just making a cruise with the old boat and it was coming up the river. They had a hard time, too, because the bushes on the banks had all grown up and the channel had filled in. I remember that they had to run a winch from the boat to trees on the bank to get it up the river, in places. Sometimes it took them two or three hours just to go a hundred yards.*

The few pages in the middle of *History and Heritage* that summarize the sparse official record of Cherokee County are about as far as any student of local history can get without mention of the ever-present Coosa River. From the 1870s through the 1910s, a few steamboats loaded with people and goods headed past on their way to Rome or Gadsden. Ferries transporting farmers and their primitive equipment floated from one bank to the other until the 1950s. If Cardon didn't mention the river too often in his 1936 article, it wasn't because it had become unimportant or he had forgotten it existed. The riverboats might have stopping steaming past but their route was still there, curving from one end of the county to the other. It's more likely the dull roar of the slow-moving Coosa was so instilled in Cardon's mind that he wouldn't have thought to mention the noise unless someone started talking about quieting it forever, and his column came twenty years too soon to document that event.

1920–1955

Cedar Bluff had a state-accredited high school in 1923, according to an article by Lucille Ringer in *History and Heritage*. By 1930, there were at least two ferries to help get the students there, but such superfluities didn't matter much in the springtime. When the Coosa swelled from the rains, like it almost always did, "the ferry was out of operation, leaving Cedar Bluff and the northern end of the county without connection with Centre and all points south of the river."

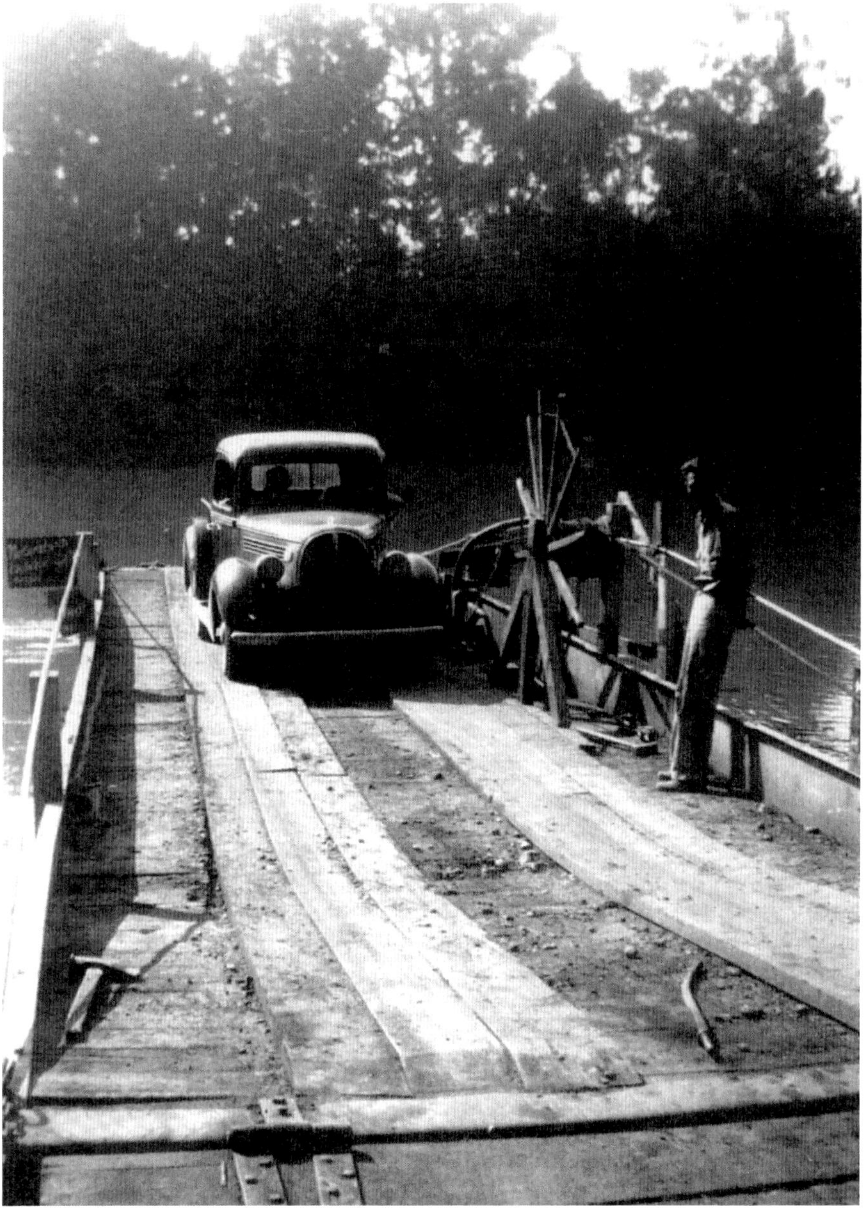

Few bridges crossed the Coosa River in Cherokee County before Weiss Lake was built. Sewell's Ferry connected the Alexis community with the town of Cedar Bluff. *Courtesy of Sue Young.*

In a series of books on the history of Cherokee County written in 1975, Colonel Robert Mann wrote extensively about the system of ferries that traversed the Coosa River. The earliest ferries, operated by settlers, resembled the boats their fathers and grandfathers copied from the Indians. Mann described them as "long logs bound together by vines or crosspieces and wooden pegs." He also included a detailed description of the next generation of ferries:

> *The first ferries of the type most older people will remember came into use after the War Between the States. They were entirely of wood construction and were propelled across the river by the force of the current against the sides of the boat. The boat was held to a fixed course by a wire rope or cable stretched across the river and usually attached to a large tree on each bank. A large windlass was provided on the side that the ferry operator used to enable him to raise or lower the wire rope or ferry line with the rise and fall of the water. The ferry was attached at either end by a rope to a pulley which ran on the ferry cable line. There was a large wheel and drum in the center of the boat on the upstream side. The ferryman, by winding the rope on the drum by hand power, could draw or place either end of the boat in a position pointing upstream. Then the ferryman, by manpower or crowbar, would pry the ferry loose from the ferry landing site, point the prow upstream, and the force of the current against the side of the boat would propel the ferry across the river. This system of propelling a boat across a stream is quite similar to "tacking" a sailboat and perhaps as old.*

Most ferries operating on the Coosa by the 1900s were equipped with hinged ramps that allowed wagons, cars or tractors to load and offload. Usually, the ferries were somewhere around fifty-five feet in length and twelve to fourteen feet wide, and they could carry a loaded wagon and a pair of two-mule teams, or three automobiles or two trucks. With a maximum load of "about twenty-five tons," Mann wrote, "the boat would draw about twenty inches of water," compared to only a six-inch draw when running empty. Mann's text listed eighteen ferries that operated at various times in Cherokee County, although he admitted his list "by no means includes all the ferries that were operated across the Coosa River during the past 140 years, only the important or better-known ferries." He attributed the information to maps he found dating back to the nineteenth century and an interview with Mr. Russell Early, who operated a ferry on the Coosa until 1973. One of the ferries on Mann's list, the Anderson Ferry connecting Centre and Leesburg, was abandoned by 1869. Another, Daniel's Ferry, which carried traffic from Yancey's Bend to Centre, "served the upper portion of the bend and was abandoned prior to 1900." Mr. Early operated his conveyance from the old Poole's Ferry location near Cedar Bluff to Williamson Island "on a private basis for growing and harvesting crops on the island."

In 1920, the county government assumed control of the ferries and paid ferrymen a flat fee of fifty dollars per month, although they could supplement their salaries by charging extra for night trips and out-of-state vehicles. On January 16, 1925, the *Coosa River News* ran a report written by ferryman Oscar Smith that documented his traffic for a twenty-four-hour period from a few days before: "109 cars, 16 trucks, 103 wagons, 12 buggies, 4 horsemen, 49 footmen."

James L. Wright grew up near the Kirk's Grove community in southeastern Cherokee County and remembered riding Sewell's Ferry to Cedar Bluff as a schoolboy in the late 1950s:

> *We'd ride the bus to school every morning, but when we got to the ferry we couldn't stay on the bus while we crossed the river. We would have to get out of the bus then wait for the driver to pull the bus onto the ferry. Then we could walk onto the ferry and ride alongside the bus until we got to the other side, in Cedar Bluff. Then the driver would pull the bus off the ferry*

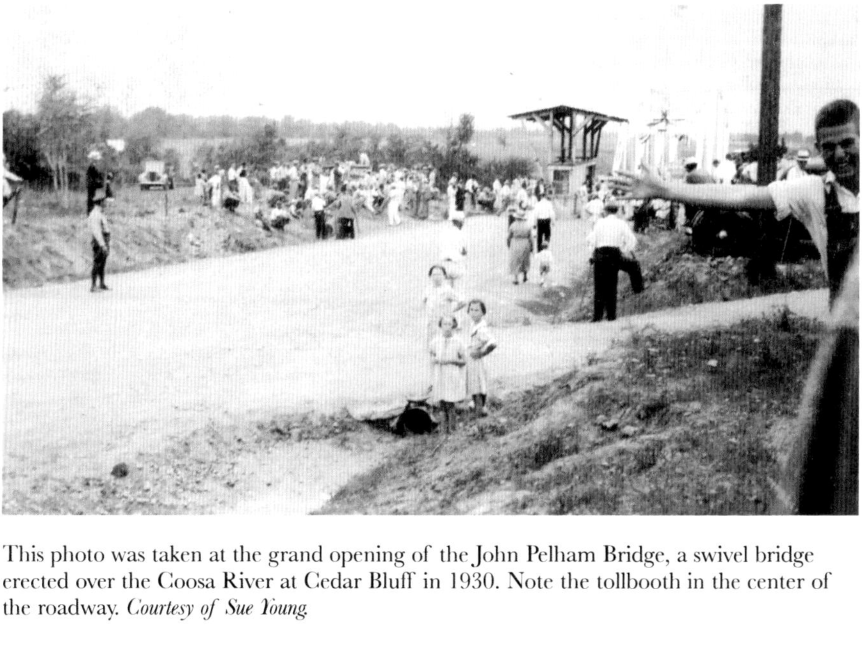

This photo was taken at the grand opening of the John Pelham Bridge, a swivel bridge erected over the Coosa River at Cedar Bluff in 1930. Note the tollbooth in the center of the roadway. *Courtesy of Sue Young.*

and we'd all get back on. We'd do it all over again on the way home that afternoon.

According to Mann, ferries began to disappear around 1920, mostly due to "the advent of the automobile and the building of many new highways, the re-routing of older roads and the building of bridges." By 1959, only Sewell's Ferry, Bradford's Ferry and Garrett's Ferry remained in operation in Cherokee County. "With the completion of Weiss Dam in 1960–61, these were discontinued," he added.

For about five years, from 1930 to 1935, at least one connection to the opposite shore didn't require passengers to exit overloaded vehicles, but they did have to pay for the convenience. The John Pelham Bridge connecting Cedar Bluff and Centre, Ringer wrote, demanded "a charge of 25 cents… for cars, buggies and wagons. This charge included the driver, but each passenger paid five cents. A horseback rider paid ten cents and a pedestrian paid five cents." The bridge, Ringer pointed out, was designed to swivel, which allowed steamboats to pass. But, she added, "this accommodation was not needed long, since sometime in the 1930s the last steamboat made its cruise." The vessel that made the last pass through Cherokee County may very well have been the same one Billy Godfrey and his classmates darted from their classroom to observe as it fought its way up the river channel.

According to Ringer, tractors and other heavy equipment made it to farms in Cherokee County by the end of World War II. These, along with other advances, altered the face of a community that had struggled to make ends meet for decades before the Great Depression came along. "With this added speed and power, along with improved seeds, machinery and knowledge of soil improvement and disease and pest controls, one person could produce more than many had been able to do in the past." Ringer wrote that men coming home from World War II often did not return to the farms. Instead, many chose to further their education or open a business. Emboldened by the experience of spending the war years in factories, many housewives decided to hire babysitters and go to work, too. With the extra money coming in, the family could afford other modern conveniences, such as washing machines or iceboxes, pre-prepared food and vegetables from someplace other than their own backyard. "This eliminated the need for the milk cow, chickens and hogs for pork," she added.

In 1952, "farming was a big business in Cherokee County," according to an article in the *Cherokee County Herald* in early 1953. County Agent J.J. Young told the newspaper that local farmers "realized a return of $6,330,000 from their investments of time and labor" during the year, an amount representing "an increase of $582,000 over 1951." Young said there were a total of 45,470 acres of row crops in the county and, "as in most Alabama counties, cotton is still king."

"The white fiber returned an estimated $4,927,000 in 1952 to farmers in Cherokee County," the article read. Corn was the number two crop in the county. Livestock was valued at $1.53 million in 1952, Young said, and the cattle and hogs grazed on a total of 28,000 acres. Another important income producer in Cherokee County in 1952 was timber, which generated an estimated $403,211. Young told the newspaper that the 1950 census estimated the average size of a farm in Cherokee County to be 100.6 acres.

As early as the late 1940s, life on the farm had begun to improve—electricity and heavy equipment made certain of that. By the time Young's 1953 annual report was released to the public, those two twentieth-century technological advances had already started to merge into a blueprint for change on an engineer's drafting table in Birmingham. By 1958, mathematical equations and blueprint sketches were on the verge of being transformed into steel and concrete. Three years later, the people of Cherokee County slowly began to realize that the prospect of letting the Coosa float them to a better future was infinitely more promising than spending their lives swimming against the slow-moving current that had long defined their past.

LOOKING TO LEESBURG

Without this legislation the Coosa River would have remained as always—a wonderful but only partially-developed stream.
—Alabama Power Company promotional booklet from the early 1960s

The Coosa River begins in Rome, Georgia, where the Oostanala and Etowah Rivers converge. Its waters meander 350 miles through the eastern half of Alabama before joining the Tallapoosa River in Montgomery to form the Alabama River. Alabama Power Company cofounders William Patrick Lay, Thomas W. Martin and James Mitchell first began discussing plans for a series of electricity-generating dams along the twisting, winding route as early as 1912. In his 1995 book, *Rivers of History: Life on the Coosa, Tallapoosa, Cahaba and Alabama*, Jacksonville State University history professor Harvey H. Jackson III thoroughly documented a century of efforts to create a navigable Coosa River channel from Rome to Wetumpka, Alabama, that began as early as 1870. Jackson also explained how each attempt foundered at the hands of miserly politicians, fickle economies or some combination of both. Year after year, the promised bevy of barges hauling cotton, livestock, corn and dozens of other products that grew in abundance along the banks of the Coosa failed to come floating past. A tricky stretch of rapidly falling river "100 miles long" between Wetumpka and Greensport, Alabama, had, by 1910, led to the virtual abandonment of efforts to dredge a passable river channel. It seemed that no one—neither state government, federal government nor private interests—felt it was their responsibility to fund the dozens of low-level dams, locks and canals required to bypass the rapids.

By 1918, the United States Congress had made a few attempts at creating a navigable channel, authorizing six separate government projects on the

Coosa River. Three series of locks were completed in different locations by 1890, with a fourth completed in 1914. Another was finished a year later at Mayo's Bar near Rome, followed by a sixth in 1918. But in 1920, the federal government surveyed the Coosa again and reported to the secretary of war—the official in charge of the nation's rivers at the time—that any further attempt to create a navigable river channel "should be abandoned due to lack of commercial use." Neglected at Uncle Sam's insistence, the locks were rendered useless over the next several years by a series of floods. After this latest, failed attempt to tame the upper Coosa, farmers had the same reaction as their fathers and grandfathers before them: they shrugged, grabbed their farming tools and returned to the fields. Cotton can't pick itself. For the next forty years, life remained unchanged for the people of Cherokee County. Farmers planted, picked and lived off the land however they could. They raised corn to feed their cows and hogs. They also sold cotton to local ginners for the money they would need to feed and clothe their families through the winter and to buy the seed and fertilizer they would need to begin the process all over again the next year.

By the mid-1930s, the nation was being pounded by the Great Depression, and Alabama Power was engaged in a fierce struggle with the Tennessee Valley Authority (TVA) for control of north Alabama waterways. President Franklin D. Roosevelt created TVA in May 1933 as part of his New Deal, and it was considered an innovative experiment in planning for the future development of the nation's rural areas, particularly the Southeast. In *Developed for the Service of Alabama: The Centennial History of the Alabama Power Company, 1906–2006*, Leah Atkins wrote that the bill creating the TVA "was the most revolutionary and the most socialistic" of FDR's New Deal projects. At the signing, Roosevelt, who had fought for months to wrest control of the nation's rivers from private companies, "looked around the room, 'made a mock inquiry for the representative of the Alabama Power Company,' and then signed the bill."

In January 1934, Alabama Power's parent company signed an agreement with TVA to purchase power from dams operated by TVA on the Tennessee River and sell various company-owned properties in Alabama, Tennessee and Mississippi. Soon afterward, thirteen Alabama Power stockholders filed suit against TVA and the company, charging that the agreement damaged the value of their holdings. Although a judge granted the stockholders an injunction, which prevented several Alabama municipalities from purchasing power from TVA, many rural customers in the state were eventually forced to choose between the federal government and the privately held, for-profit company for their electricity needs. Several cities in Alabama and Mississippi

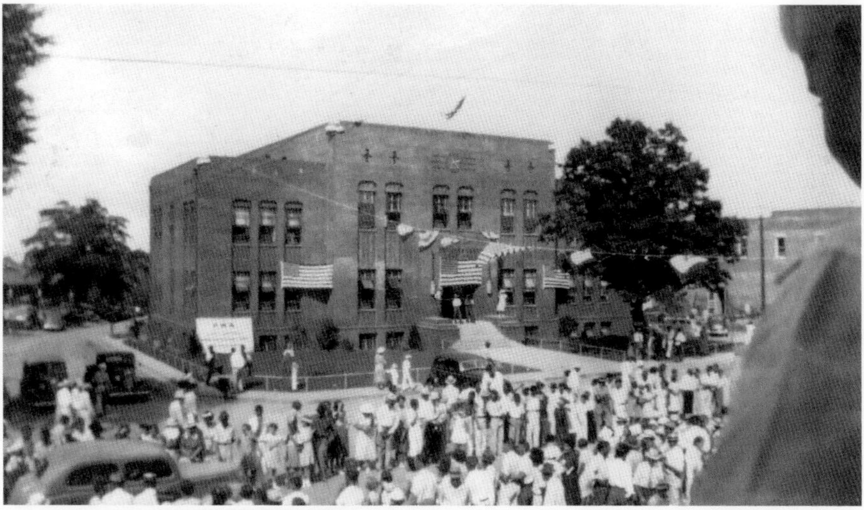

A crowd of hundreds gathered in Centre to celebrate Cherokee County's centennial in 1936. Around the same time, TVA began supplying electricity to homes in the area. *Courtesy of Gadsden Public Library.*

held public elections to choose a supplier. In Scottsboro, Atkins wrote, TVA crews installed power lines down one side of the street at the same time Alabama Power crews were removing poles and lines from the other. A U.S. Supreme Court decision in May 1936 forced Alabama Power to transfer fourteen cities and Wheeler Dam to TVA control. In response to TVA's growing monopoly, over a dozen electric utilities in eastern Tennessee filed suit to prevent TVA from assuming control of their facilities.

The fight with TVA, Atkins wrote, "produced uncertainty and poor publicity" for Alabama Power that lasted for years. The conflict over customers continued sporadically until 1940 and did not officially end until passage of the TVA Financing Act of 1959, when the southern boundary of Cherokee County effectively became a Mason-Dixon line between the two entities. That truce is the explanation for why, to this day, little if any of the electricity generated by Weiss Dam powers refrigerators and satellite receivers in Cherokee County. The Cherokee Electric Cooperative, which supplies every home and business in a county defined by an Alabama Power–owned reservoir, purchases its electricity directly from TVA.

In many ways, it was the beginning of World War II that allowed the construction of Weiss Dam to begin seventeen years later. Hydroelectric TVA power plants had begun popping up just before the war, in part because of a secret Federal Power Commission report compiled in 1938. The report

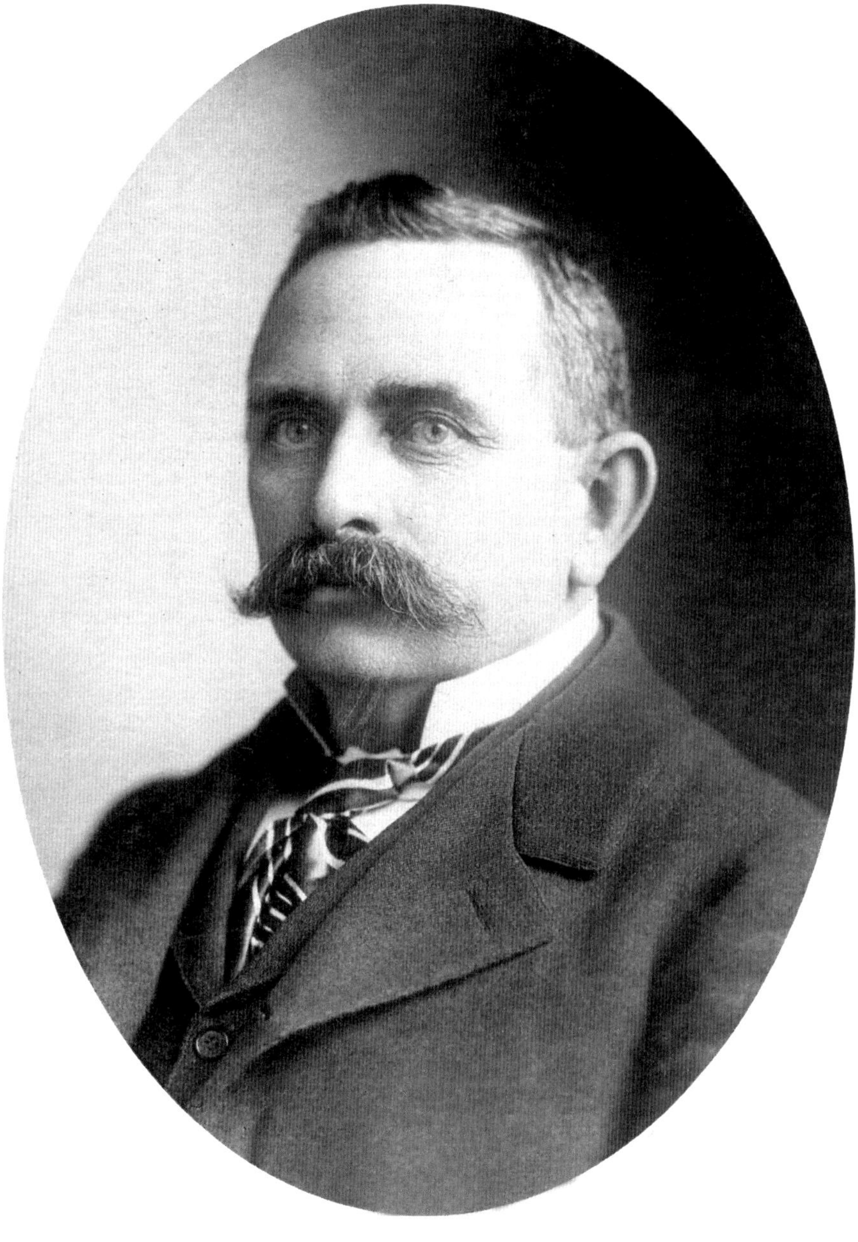

John L. Burnett, the only Cherokee County native ever elected to the United States Congress, was born in Cedar Bluff on January 20, 1854. He served in Congress from 1899 until his death in 1919. *Courtesy of the National Archives.*

predicted the nation would soon face severe shortages of electricity that should be addressed before the war started, rather than after. When the war ended in August 1945, the eight or nine million men and women who had served in the United States military began coming back from Europe and the Pacific with a newfound appreciation for how electricity could improve their way of life at home. For many of them, returning to unlit towns and farmhouses was a step backward. An economic boom in mid-1946, fueled by federal home construction loan programs for veterans, soon had both TVA and Alabama Power scrambling to erect power lines and generate the additional kilowatts that thousands of new rural customers were beginning to demand.

Years before, the call for electricity in Alabama, as well as Alabama Power's ability to raise construction capital from investors, had dropped off significantly as the country suffered through the Great Depression. The dams already in operation along the lower half of the Coosa were sufficient to supply all the electricity Alabama Power could profitably sell during lean times. One of those dams was the Lock 12 dam, later renamed Lay Dam, which was completed in 1914. The bill authorizing that project was introduced by John L. Burnett, the only Cherokee County native ever elected to the United States Congress. President Theodore Roosevelt signed Burnett's bill into law in March 1907, and seven years later the Lock 12 dam became the state's first major hydroelectric generating plant. Forty years passed before the legislation that eventually made Weiss Dam possible was introduced by Representative Albert Rains of Gadsden. An Alabama Power promotional booklet from the early 1960s declared that, without the legislation introduced by Rains, "the Coosa River would have remained as always—a wonderful but only partially-developed stream." Another survey of the river by the U.S. Army Corps of Engineers, completed in 1953, had trimmed the number of dams the federal government considered necessary for navigation and flood control from over thirty to eight. With three already in place, Alabama Power stood ready to initiate a vast construction plan that would erect the remaining five.

By the early 1940s, TVA was using the waterways of north Alabama to generate electricity for the war effort and stifling private energy interests in the region, Alabama Power in particular. For a time, after World War II ended in 1945, there was talk in Washington of expanding TVA operations south to the Coosa River, but federal funding was scarce during the administration of President Harry S. Truman. In 1953, Truman's successor, General Dwight D. Eisenhower, took a stance against the Tennessee Valley Authority or any further expansion of taxpayer-funded power production. It was Eisenhower's

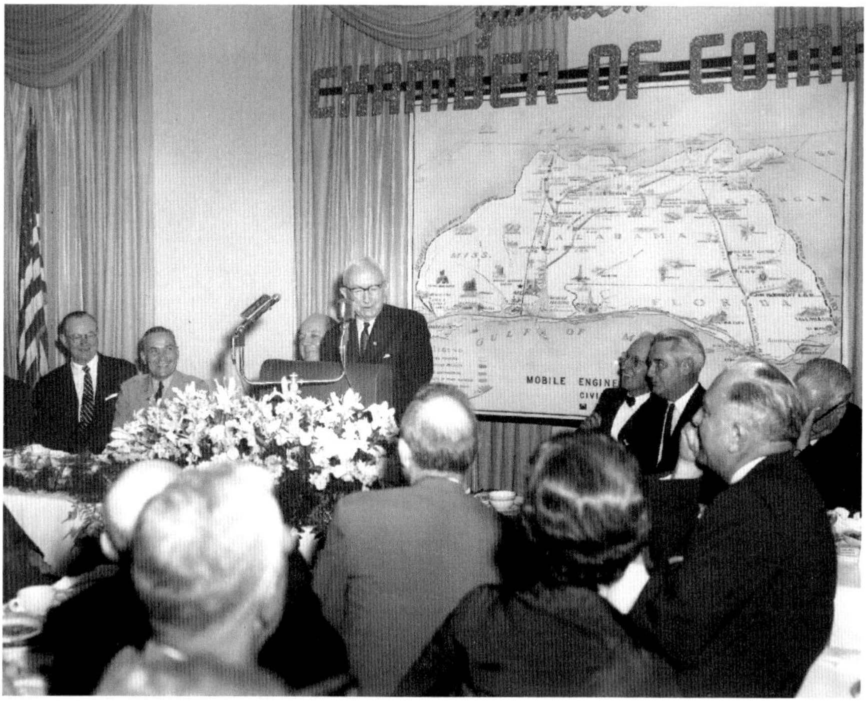

Alabama Power Co. Chairman Thomas W. Martin speaks to the Centre Chamber of Commerce the night before the groundbreaking ceremony in Leesburg in April 1958. Martin led the company's efforts to build a series of dams on the upper Coosa River. *Courtesy of Alabama Power Company.*

resistance to the southerly spread of TVA that provided the opportunity for Alabama Power to realize its long-held vision for the Coosa.

With a small-government conservative like Ike in the White House, Alabama Power officials, led by Martin, began talking about renewing the company's plans for the continued development of the Coosa. As Atkins wrote, soon after Eisenhower took office, Martin "began to push the company's plan for more Coosa River dams." The first hurdle Martin had to clear was Alabama's delegation in the United States Congress. Senators Lister Hill and John Sparkman both favored government-funded, Democrat-created New Deal programs like TVA. Both, however, were also vocal advocates of industrial expansion in Alabama. Martin knew he would have to approach Hill and Sparkman with a plan that allowed privately owned dams on the Coosa, while also appealing to the senators' sense of service to the public good. The bill Representative Rains introduced in 1954 was eventually crafted into language deemed satisfactory by both senators.

On November 12, 1953, Alabama Power filed an application with the Federal Power Commission requesting permission to build four new dams on the Coosa River and make modifications to Lock 12. After spending months poring over maps, old river surveys and decades of company records on water flows and flood data, company engineers selected what they considered ideal spots for the new dams near the Alabama towns of Leesburg, Ragland, Vincent and Clanton. One potential holdup for the project, Atkins wrote, was a Rivers and Harbor Act passed by Congress in 1945. The law had "staked out the Coosa for public power projects and suspended the authority of the Federal Power Commission to authorize any new private construction." Negotiations between Alabama Power officials and politicians in Washington, D.C., including senators Hill and Sparkman, led to a compromise version of the Rains bill that was signed into law by Eisenhower on June 28, 1954. With the law's passing, Alabama Power received permission to build the dams in exchange for a promise to renegotiate contracts and provide electricity at discounted rates to the dozen or so rural cooperatives that they already supplied. The company was also required to implement a comprehensive river development plan created the year before by the U.S. Army Corps of Engineers (following yet another survey of the Coosa). As a result of the agreement, Alabama Power became responsible for flood control, as well as providing nine-foot-deep channels and including accommodations for a series of navigation locks, in case the government should ever provide the millions of federal dollars it would take to open the river to barge traffic.

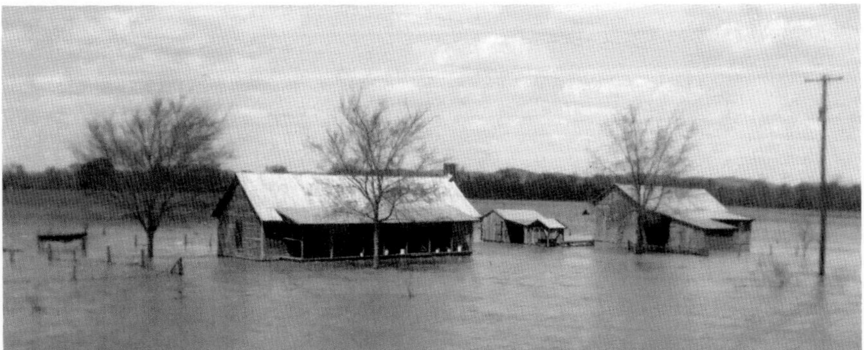

Localized floods known as "backwaters" were typical in the springtime along the banks of the Coosa River before Weiss Lake was constructed. *Courtesy of Sue Young.*

The legislation signed by President Eisenhower had one other important stipulation. From the day it was signed, Alabama Power had exactly ten years to complete work at all five sites. As Atkins pointed out, twenty-five years had passed since Alabama Power completed its last major dam construction project. If the company hoped to build $120 million worth of hydroelectric generating power and tame practically an entire 350-mile river in less than a decade, it was going to require the services of an engineering genius with decades of dam-building experience. Luckily, the right man for the job was sitting at a desk in a practically empty office in downtown Birmingham. He was already on the Alabama Power payroll, too, and had been for over forty years.

THE LAKE'S NAMESAKE

He is an engineer with imagination. Even rarer, he has the ability to imbue other men with that imagination.

—Walter Bouldin, speaking about Fernand C. Weiss, April 26, 1958

In June 1954, when Alabama Power won federal approval to build a series of dams on the upper Coosa River, an entire generation had passed since the company finished its last major dam-construction project. The company spent little money on construction during the Depression years and maintained only a skeleton staff in its engineering department through World War II, according to documents in the company archives. Fortunately for Alabama Power, at least one of the engineers still on staff remembered where he kept his slide rule.

Fernand C. Weiss was born in Dallas, Texas, on March 5, 1892. After graduating from high school, he attended the University of Texas before transferring to the Massachusetts Institute of Technology, where he earned a degree in electrical engineering. He was hired by Alabama Power to string transmission lines shortly after completing his train ride home in 1913. According to a memorial written by the company after his death, Weiss exhibited "industry, an ability to get things done, and excellent technical qualifications"—the exact attributes, it turned out, that a company run by a visionary like Thomas W. Martin was looking for. Very quickly, the memorial read, Weiss "attracted the attention of his supervisors." He saw his responsibility within the company expand quickly, and by the time of his passing, he had progressed "steadily until he became the chief executive of the company in the engineering and construction fields."

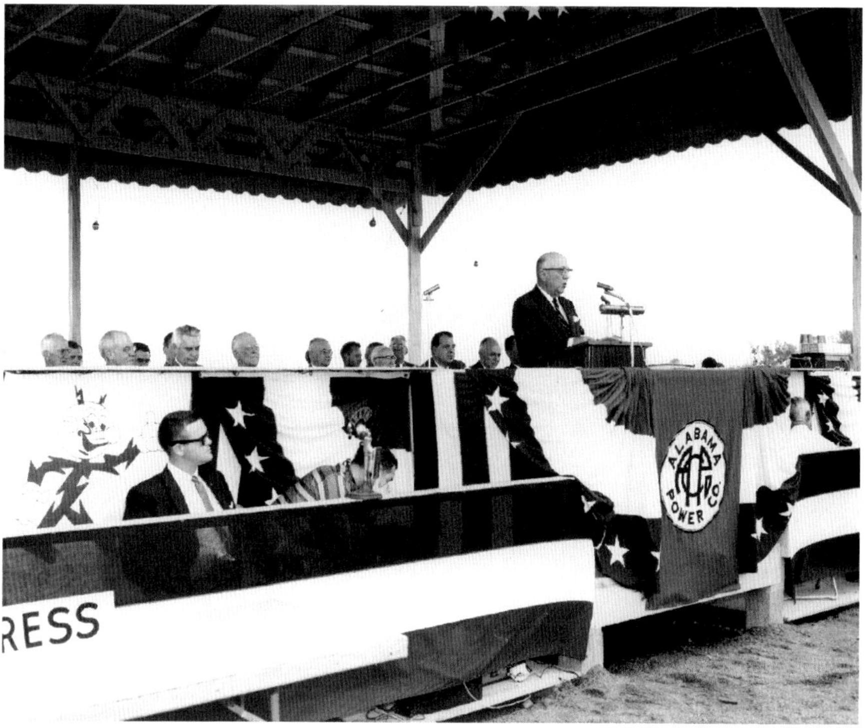

Fernand C. Weiss speaks at the groundbreaking for the Leesburg project on April 26, 1958. *Courtesy of Alabama Power Company.*

Weiss became a construction superintendent in 1915 and over the next twenty-six years helped build four dams on the lower Coosa and Tallapoosa Rivers. From 1918 to 1931, he was one of the leaders of Dixie Construction Company and Allied Engineers, Inc., both affiliates of Alabama Power at the time. After the federal government forced the company to spin off its construction interests in 1931, Weiss became the construction manager for Alabama Power. He was elected vice president in charge of engineering and construction ten years later and became a director in 1956.

Weiss, a dead ringer for Alfred Hitchcock in his later years, actually retired from Alabama Power a few weeks before the groundbreaking for Weiss Dam on April 26, 1958. On April 1, after forty-five years of figuring, designing and building, Weiss officially stepped down. The board of directors adopted a resolution "acknowledging his lasting contribution woven into the efficient plants and transmission systems of the Company; and that his contribution will continue on through the years through the competent and able associates he gathered together and welded into an outstanding staff."

Weiss's knowledge of ongoing company projects on the upper Coosa meant he would stay on as the head of a group of supervising consultants. (There is no one left at Alabama Power who knew him so the question cannot be answered with certainty, but possibly the fact that the company's new $30 million dam in Leesburg would bear his name helped persuade Weiss to stay on the job a little longer.)

Among the major construction projects Weiss oversaw during his four-decade career were a steam plant near Chickasaw, the Barry Steam Plant and Gorgas Steam Plants Nos. 2 and 3. He was also responsible for designing the "intricate system of transmission lines radiating from them." Sadly, Weiss would not live to see his namesake completed. The June 1959 issue of *Powergrams*, Alabama Power's monthly news magazine, announced Weiss's passing on May 30. "With the simple dignity that characterized him during his lifetime, Fernand C. Weiss was laid to his final rest in Elmwood Cemetery in Birmingham, Alabama." According to the obituary, Weiss fell ill only a few days before he died. The cause of his death, at age sixty-six, was not noted. The obituary listed Weiss's affiliations, including membership in the Scottish Rite Masons and the Theta Xi fraternity. He was also a member of the Birmingham Chamber of Commerce, the Downtown Club, the American Institute of Electrical Engineers, the Engineers Club of Birmingham, the Society of Professional Engineers and the Southern Skeet Club.

Informed of the death of his longtime friend and co-worker, Martin, Alabama Power's chairman of the board, emitted a mouthful in remembrance: "His genius will be sorely missed but his sound engineering judgment led him to organize and train a capable staff which will execute brilliantly in every complexity the program with which he had been closely identified." A year earlier at the Leesburg groundbreaking, with Weiss seated on the dais, Alabama Power President Walter Bouldin began a chorus of praise that lasted well over an hour. Bouldin called Weiss "more than a great builder; he is an engineer with imagination. Even rarer, he has the ability to imbue other men with that imagination." Congressman Armistead I. Selden called the naming of the reservoir in honor of Weiss "a splendid tribute to an outstanding engineer." Congressman Frank Boykin commended the decision to name the project for Weiss, telling the overflow crowd that Weiss's "engineering skill and broad vision have made possible a plan which will provide for the comprehensive development for the Coosa River."

There were only a handful of pictures of Weiss in the Alabama Power archives, two of which appear in this publication for the first time. In one picture, a young, wide-eyed Weiss, probably about six years old, posed for a photo wearing the long hair and sailor suit people snicker at today but

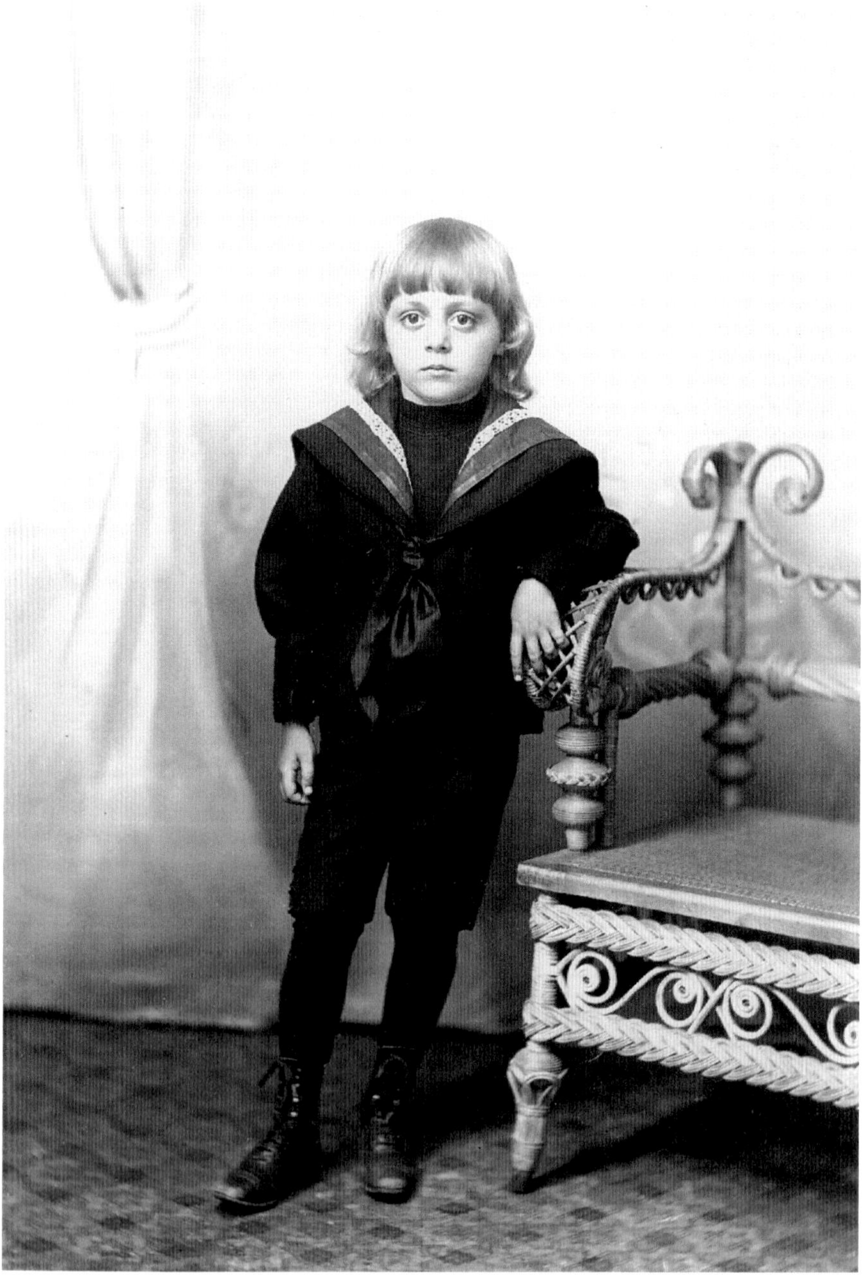

Photo circa 1898. Weiss would have been about six years old at this time. *Courtesy of Alabama Power Company.*

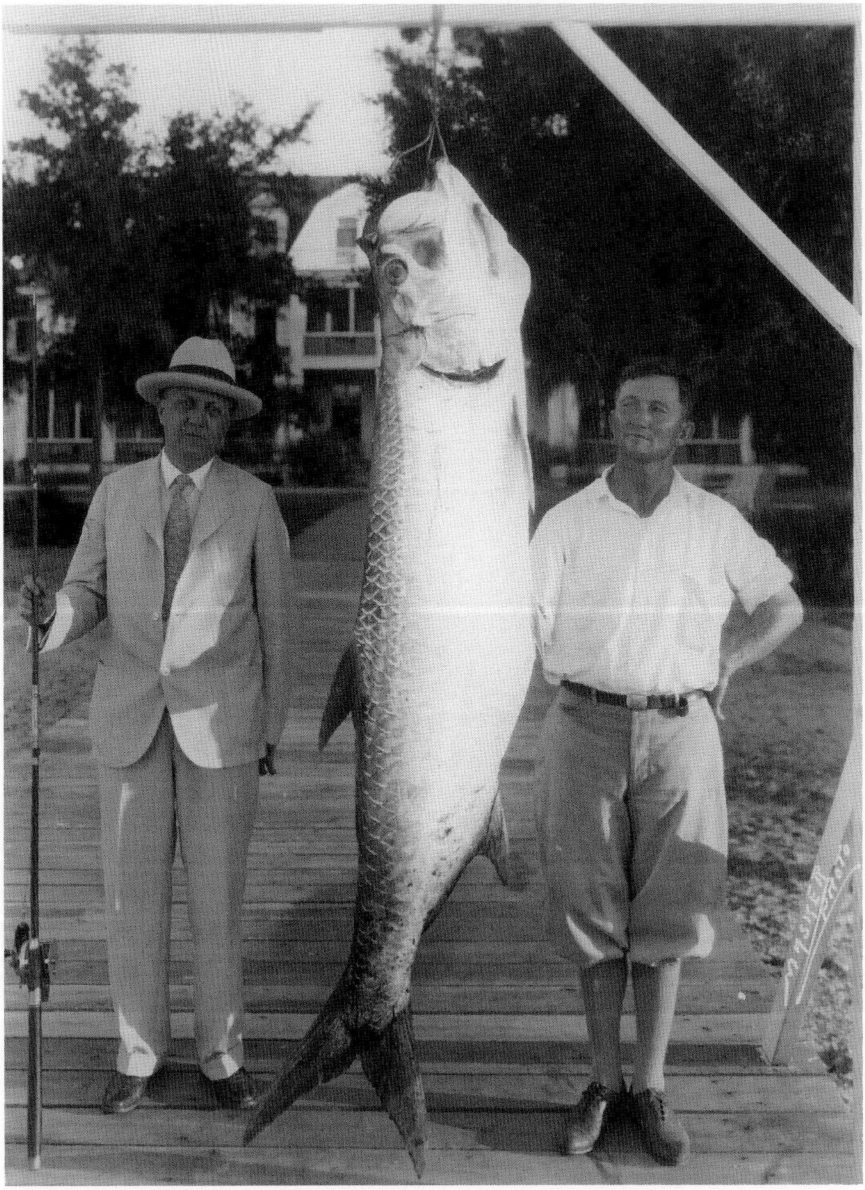

Photo circa 1932. Weiss (at left) was an avid sportsman who enjoyed skeet shooting and fishing. *Courtesy of Alabama Power Company.*

mothers must have insisted looked manly and handsome a century ago. In another, from the early 1930s, Weiss posed in a three-piece white suit complete with fedora alongside a huge tarpon he reeled in during a fishing trip to Panama City Beach, Florida.

Considering Weiss's apparent love for fishing, it seems appropriate that his name graces the reservoir the Cherokee County Chamber of Commerce proudly advertises across the nation today as "the Crappie Capital of the World." No close relatives survived Weiss, the obituary in *Powergrams* noted, but "hundreds of friends paid tribute by their presence" at the graveside service. Fifty years later, considering all the friends and families who regularly gather to splash, fish and play in the lake named in his honor, the number of people who have paid tribute to the memory of Fernand C. Weiss is well into the hundreds of thousands.

CHANGES ON THE WAY

Whatever prosperity Cherokee County has enjoyed since it was first settled has been due to its agriculture and nothing else. When thousands of acres of productive farm land [are] permanently destroyed, what happens then to the economy of Cherokee County? The answer is simple and obvious, ruination and bankruptcy.
—Tom Burke, letter to the editor, February 1956

It took contractors working for Alabama Power less time to move the millions of cubic yards of earth and pour the hundreds of thousands of yards of concrete that compose Weiss Dam than it took federal and state officials to grant the company permission to begin construction. Alabama Power filed the application to complete its development plan of the Coosa River on November 12, 1953. A law signed by President Dwight D. Eisenhower in June 1954 granted permission to proceed with the next step in the process, and Alabama Power sought consent from the Alabama Public Service Commission on December 2, 1955. The state granted the necessary certificate of convenience two months later. Finally, in September 1957, the Federal Power Commission removed the last obstacle. In all, it took two months shy of four years for Alabama Power to untangle itself from a ream of government red tape.

Within seven months of the FPC decision, the company held a massive groundbreaking near the dam site in Leesburg, complete with pyrotechnics, a barbecue lunch for over ten thousand, a tanker truck full of Meadow Gold ice cream and a stage filled with hand-pumping politicians ready to take credit for the entire affair. Amidst the throng was the unpretentious, reserved Fernand C. Weiss, who by all accounts had earned the right to have his name attached to what would become his final engineering project.

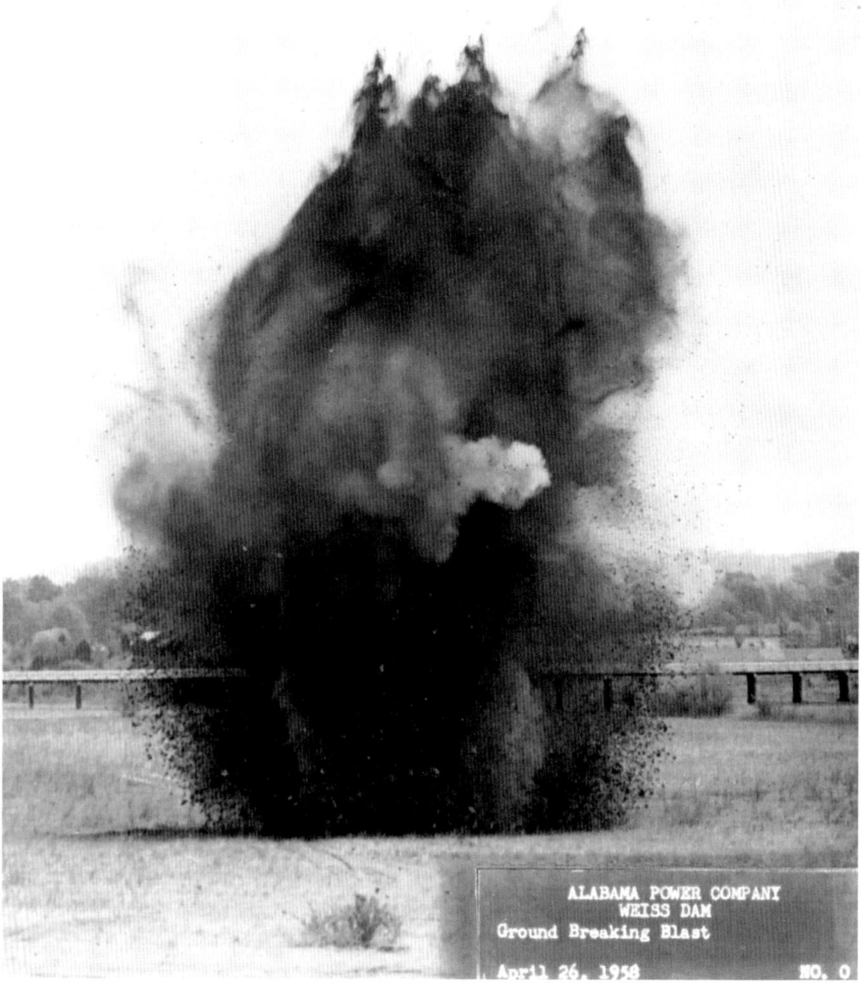

The groundbreaking concluded with a ceremonial blast of dynamite near the future spillway construction site. *Courtesy of Alabama Power Company.*

From the day they received the go-ahead, engineers and construction workers were able to erect a ninety-foot-high concrete dam and massive powerhouse, complete with three thirty-nine-thousand-horsepower turbines each capable of generating twenty-eight thousand kilowatts of electricity. They did it all in just over three years, and that includes the time it took to clean and cook the hogs the company barbecued and served in Leesburg on April 26. Construction of Weiss Dam officially began two months later, on July 31, 1958, and the facility went into service on June 5, 1961. It's almost

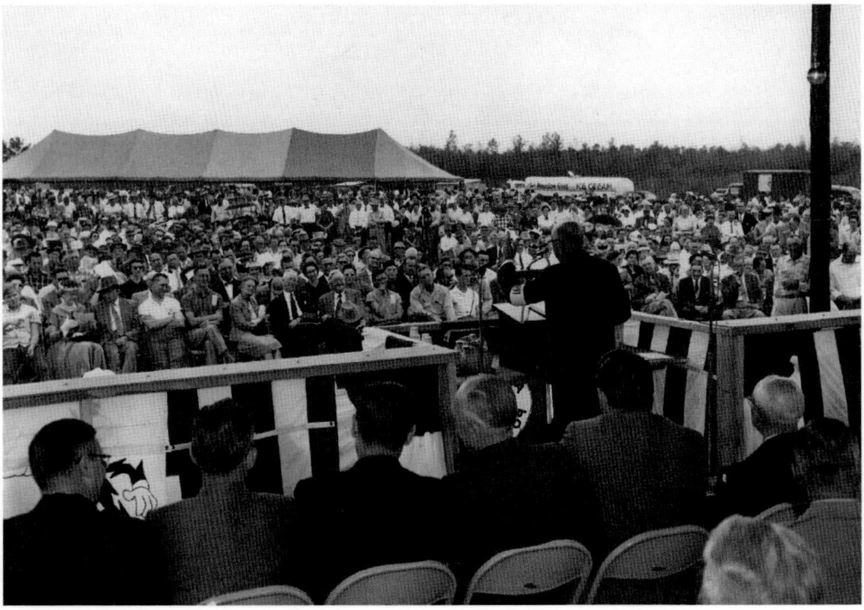

Newspaper accounts of the groundbreaking estimated that around twelve thousand people attended the event. Hopefully, there was enough Meadow Gold ice cream to go around. *Courtesy of Alabama Power Company.*

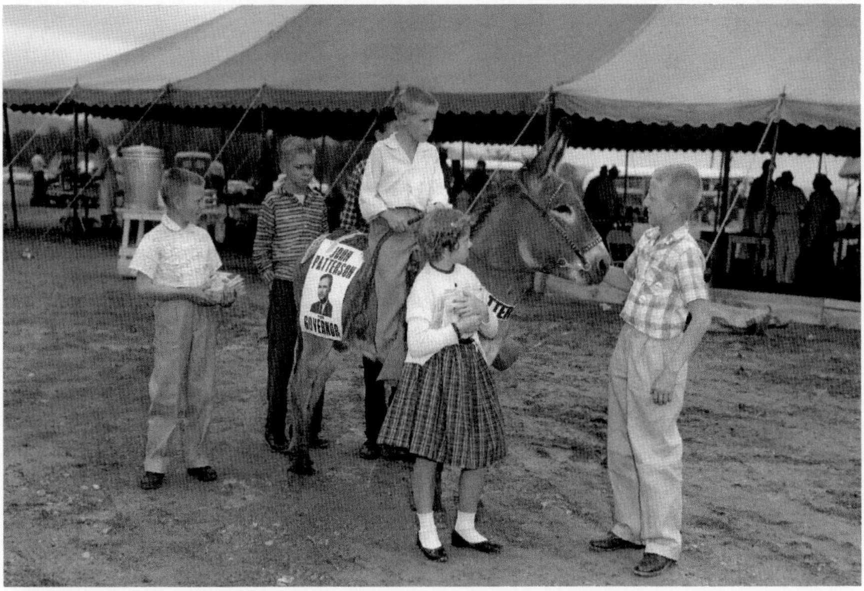

The dais at the groundbreaking was filled with politicians and their spokesmen. Here, children get a closer look at the Alabama governor's chosen representative. *Courtesy of Alabama Power Company.*

enough to make a person wonder what the folks in Scottsboro were thinking in the 1930s, when they chose the lumbering, government-run TVA for their electricity provider when a go-getter like Alabama Power was their other option.

An article in the *Gadsden Times* reported that Alabama Power Chairman of the Board Thomas W. Martin announced that contracts for construction of Weiss Dam and Reservoir were let in June 1958. Morrison-Knudsen, Inc. of Boise, Idaho, and Moss-Thorton, Inc. of Leeds, Alabama, were awarded the initial $9.5 million contract to "build the diversion dam, powerhouse structure, dikes and canals and related facilities of the dam." Alabama Power had already purchased over $7 million worth of electrical equipment, which was scheduled to be delivered to the construction site at the appropriate stages. Plans for the dam also called for the relocation of millions of yards of earth that would be piled and compressed to form miles-long dikes designed to impede and divert the Coosa River and 143,000 cubic yards of concrete for the spillway dam and powerhouse. Total cost for the construction of Weiss Dam was estimated at $30 million (the final bill was closer to $35 million). Among the projected costs were $7.57 million for land and land rights, $3.43 million for bridges and raised roadways, $11.5 million for the dam and powerhouse, $6.1 million for turbines and generators, $499,000 for transmission facilities and over $1 million in other spending for "accessories and miscellaneous power equipment." The company's statewide construction budget for 1958 was over $47 million, a 50 percent increase over the previous year, according to a story in a Birmingham newspaper. "The board's approval of this record construction budget is ample evidence of confidence that greatly expanded power facilities will be needed in Alabama in the ensuing years," Martin told the *Post-Herald*. By 1959, as work at Leesburg and other dam sites along the Coosa progressed, the company's construction budget climbed to $55 million.

In 1956, Morrison-Knudsen (M-K) was the largest construction company in the world. According to the company's internal monthly magazine, *The Em-Kayan*, while the dam in Leesburg was commencing, crews working under the M-K umbrella were simultaneously constructing a $17 million dam on the Little Red River in Arkansas, underground silos for the United States Air Force's Titan missile in Altus, Oklahoma, and a thirteen-mile-long rock, sand and gravel causeway across Utah's Great Salt Lake. Moss-Thorton was well known in the South and specialized in earthmoving and asphalt. (In the late 1960s, the company shaped and formed the massive piles of earth that today compose the thirty-three-degree banked turns of Talladega Superspeedway, a little over an hour south of Centre near Anniston.)

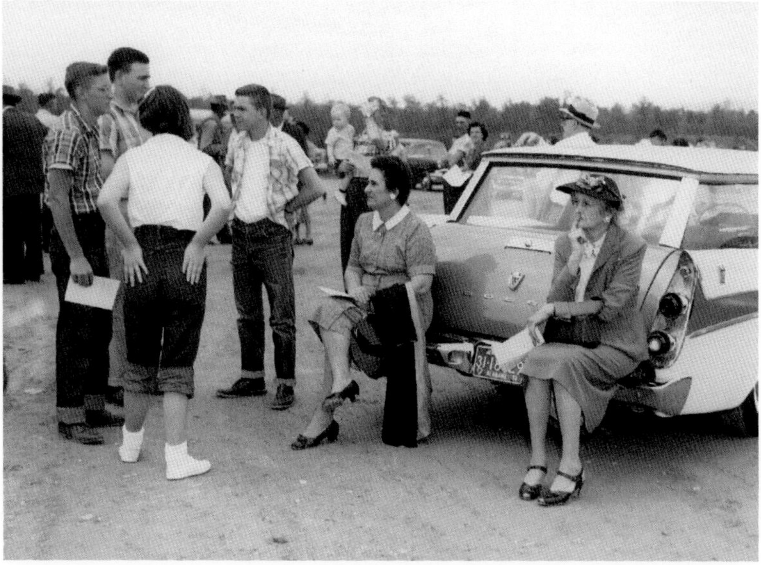

Not everyone who attended the Leesburg groundbreaking thought the flooding of thirty thousand acres of prime farmland was a good idea. *Courtesy of Alabama Power Company.*

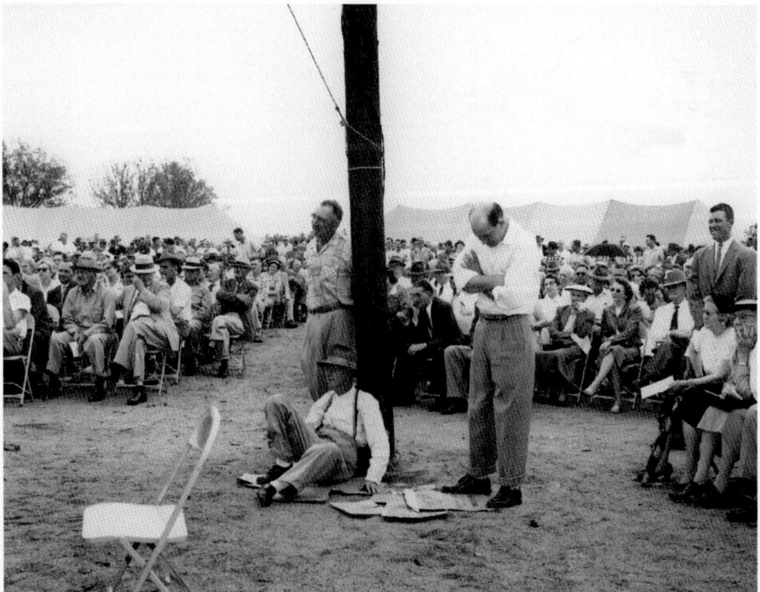

Local students helped serve over ten thousand plates of barbecue at the Weiss Dam groundbreaking, and four high school bands entertained a standing-room-only crowd. *Courtesy of Alabama Power Company.*

Articles from various newspapers often repeated the same, company-supplied statistics about the particulars of Weiss Dam. Stories often referred to the "unusual design," which consisted of a spillway dam in one location and a powerhouse four miles away. They were connected by a man-made canal "approximately two miles long." The canal was to be "over 25 feet deep, and end in a lake of approximately two square miles on the edge of which the power plant will be." There was a reason for the unique design of the construction project in Leesburg, as Dr. Harvey H. Jackson III described in *Rivers of History: Life on the Coosa, Tallapoosa, Cahaba and Alabama*. He helped readers visualize the Coosa River and its northern stretches this way: "Unhurried by gravity, it went around obstacles rather than over them, and in the first two hundred miles of its meanderings, cut a course twice as long as it would have needed had it flowed in a straight line." Jackson noted that early settlers claimed that the Coosa "curved to touch every farm in the valley."

It was at the open end of one of those long, horseshoe-shaped curves where engineers decided to block the flow of the river channel and divert it directly from one end of the horseshoe to the other, cutting out the twenty-mile loop in between. Since the Coosa dropped almost a foot for every mile it traveled as it wound its way through Cherokee County, the dam would add almost twenty feet to the river's flow at the powerhouse, creating a fifty-five-foot wall of water that Alabama Power could harness to spin three giant turbines and generate electricity for little more than the cost of construction and routine maintenance. After passing through the turbines and into a collection area known as the tailrace, the water would divert into the powerhouse and then be redirected into the original channel. From there, the river would continue toward Gadsden and eventually into the next man-made reservoir in the chain of lakes Alabama Power had planned for the upper half of the Coosa.

In another Alabama Power press release that appeared in several area newspapers in the months before construction began, F.C. Weiss laid out more construction statistics associated with the project, including the requirement of 6.5 million cubic yards of earth for the estimated six miles of diversionary dikes emanating from the powerhouse. The eastern earth dike, Weiss explained, would run 8,890 feet and the western dike 9,770 feet; two others totaled over 11,000 feet in length. The results of the impoundment, read several identical articles, would be a "lake created by the damming of the river that will be approximately 45 square miles in area and will provide many excellent sites for cottages, fishing, boating and other outdoor sports."

As was often the case, since Alabama Power and elected officials were actively seeking public approval for the project, there was frequent mention of the long-promised navigation locks. In a June 1957 article in the *Gadsden Times*, staff writer Al Fox wrote that he had spoken with Albert Rains about the navigational aspects of the Leesburg project. Three years earlier, it had been Rains who introduced the bill in Congress that ultimately became the law granting Alabama Power permission to pursue its plan to dam the upper Coosa. Rains told Fox the final approval to begin the project was expected to come from the Federal Power Commission "in the very near future." He also spouted the standard line regarding the locks. When asked about an upcoming traffic survey of the Coosa-Alabama Rivers, Rains replied, "If that report is favorable, and we anticipate it will be, we will immediately ask Congress for the money to begin construction of the dams below Montgomery and to install navigation locks at the same time the power company dams are built."

Maybe Rains still believed the story he was telling in the late 1950s, but after a hundred years of unkept promises and unrealized dreams, few people in Cherokee County believed they'd ever see barges floating up and down the Coosa River. In a letter to the editor published in 1955, Centre resident Howard Boatfield made it clear that he was insulted by the efforts of Rains and power company officials to sell the dam as a way to open the river to barge traffic: "Does [Alabama Power] think that because we are country people, that we believe the power company's propaganda about navigation on the Coosa River?"

Even with the government hurdles cleared and the yarn about the locks spun another time, Alabama Power still had to battle a group from Cherokee County, led by Boatfield and other farmers, who vehemently opposed construction of the lake. Depending on the newspaper columnist, the Coosa River Valley Land Protective Association (CRVLPA) consisted of between a few dozen and several hundred members in the mid-1950s. The group was organized by a collection of farmers and cotton ginners determined to try and prevent the construction of Weiss Dam, which, if built as conceived, would flood thousands of acres of the county's most valuable farmland. In a 1956 letter to the *Gadsden Times*, Mrs. Gladys Barnes of Route 2, Centre, was critical of the lack of support the newly formed CRVLPA had received from the paper's editorial board. She wrote:

> *Recently in an editorial, the Land Protective Association was given undue criticism on their stand against flooding a major part of the Cherokees* [sic] *rich farm lands. Yes, Mr. Editor, we are for progress, if any of that*

> *progress was for Cherokee. But all we get is a weakened economy with thousands of our people made homeless and jobless and the loss of our personal property rights.*

Cedar Bluff resident Nathan Pearson echoed those sentiments in another letter to the *Times*, written in reply to an editorial that appeared in the paper on February 2, 1956:

> *I feel you have given a distorted and unfair judgment of a group of citizens fighting a desperate battle to save the homes and land which we love and upon which we are dependent for our livelihood. All most of the people in this area know is that* [the plan] *has been masked in mystery and cloaked in secrecy.*

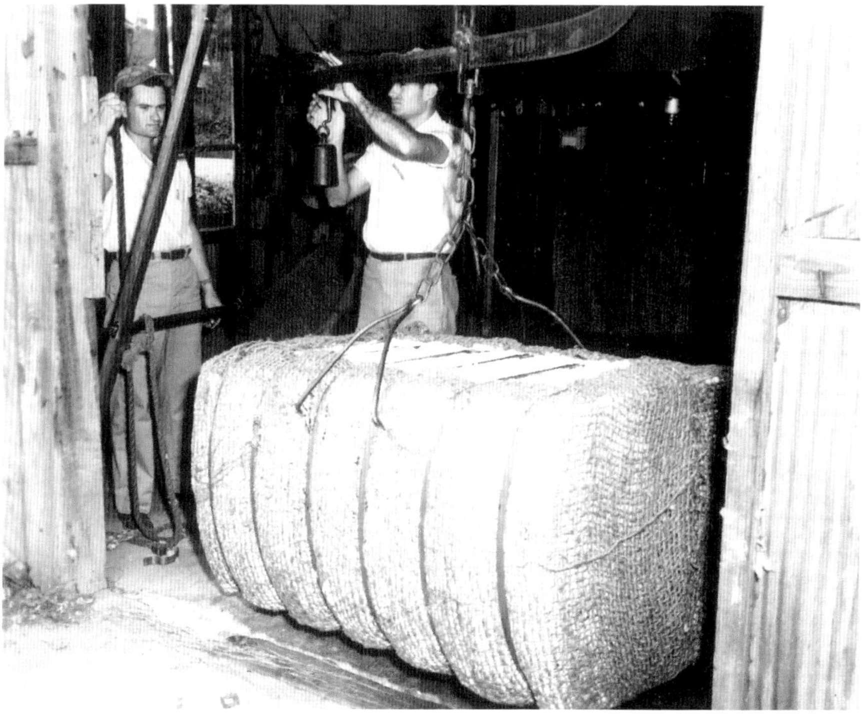

Forrest (left) and Nathan Pearson operated a cotton gin in Cedar Bluff. The brothers traveled from Montgomery to Washington, D.C., in the late 1950s to try and prevent Alabama Power from flooding their neighbors' farms. *Courtesy of Doris Pearson.*

In a letter to the *Cherokee County Herald*, Tom Burke lamented that

> *whatever prosperity Cherokee County has enjoyed since it was first settled has been due to its agriculture and nothing else. When thousands of acres of productive farm land* [are] *permanently destroyed, what happens then to the economy of Cherokee County? The answer is simple and obvious, ruination and bankruptcy.*

It often seemed to members of the CRVLPA that just about everyone, including members of the media, was helping Alabama Power stack the deck in favor of the dam project. CRVLPA literature of the day claimed that 1,500 families and a total of 7,350 people in Cherokee County would be directly affected by the construction. They urged Alabama Power to consider lower-level dams that would save more farmland, or build a steam plant to generate electricity. Conversely, documents presented to the Public Service Commission by Alabama Power at a hearing in January 1956 estimated that only 327 homes would be affected by construction of the reservoir; of those, the company claimed, thirteen were vacant and another forty were completely abandoned.

Forrest Pearson, who worked at his father's cotton gin in Cedar Bluff with his brothers Nathan and David, was one of the founding members of the CRVLPA. If the lake came, they figured they were likely to see many of their customers' cotton fields washed away. So the Pearson boys quickly took up the fight to preserve the family's way of life:

> *There were about five of us to begin with. We were the only cotton ginners and the others were farmers. We all got to talking, wondering if there was anything we could do to stop them from building the lake. I remember that we had a meeting at the old Cedar Bluff Bank, and we hashed the whole thing up one side and down the other and decided we were going to try and fight the power company.*

Following the decision to stand their ground, literally, members of the CRVLPA traveled to Rome to speak with a friend of one in the group who was an attorney. "He told us that since the thing was happening in Alabama, it would be better if we got an attorney in Alabama," Pearson said. So they headed off in the opposite direction, down Highway 11 to Birmingham.

> *About that time, Mr. and Mrs. Robert Mann got involved, and he knew from experience fighting with telephone companies in New York that a small*

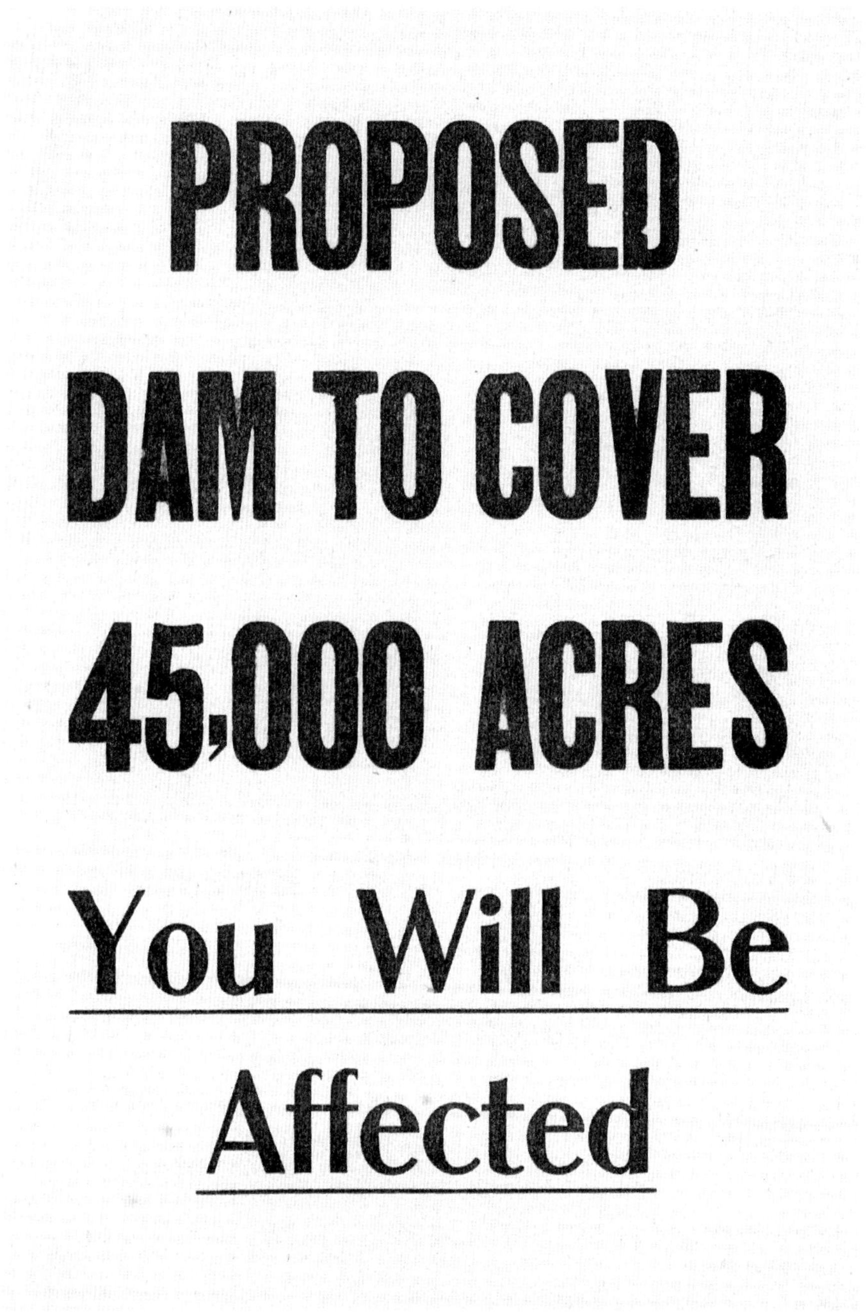

This page and next: As these fliers attest, the Coosa River Valley Land Protective Association fought vigorously to stop the condemnation of Cherokee County's best farmland for the construction of Weiss Lake. *Courtesy of the Cherokee County Public Library.*

WE HAVE PROTESTED
AT MONTGOMERY

•

WE ARE PROTESTING
IN WASHINGTON

•

THESE PROTESTS ARE FOR THE BENEFIT OF ALL TO BE AFFECTED BY THE PROPOSED DAM IN CHEROKEE COUNTY

Contact A Representative Of The

Coosa River Valley Land Protective Association

T O D A Y

group of people like us could just aggravate the soup out of one of these major companies. He said they always feared an uprising.

The CRVLPA fought Alabama Power as best it could. The group ran newspaper advertisements warning landowners to resist selling their property until the Federal Power Commission made the final decision on the dam. Members also wrote dozens of letters to newspapers across the state seeking support. In February 1956, Pearson and other CRVLPA members traveled to Montgomery to argue their case. Ultimately, the Alabama Public Service Commission (PSC) saw little harm in the project and approved Alabama Power's construction plans. According to the *Birmingham Post-Herald*, the PSC felt that the newly created lake would "result in the taking of less land than any other feasible alternative scheme by development." So the commission approved the project, which, in its opinion, "provides benefits substantially in excess of its cost or the cost of providing the same benefits by alternative methods…We conclude that the private rights in the lands involved here must be relinquished in the public interest." The State of Alabama decided their farms would have to go, but CRVLPA members weren't tired of fighting, at least not yet. "Even after the hearing in front of the state Public Service Commission in Montgomery, we didn't give up," Pearson said.

Alabama Power officials had worked hard for years to sell the idea of a massive, permanent flood to the people of Cherokee County and, judging by newspaper coverage of the time, the plan was generally well received, despite the efforts of the CRVLPA. An article in the *Cherokee County Herald* from 1955, before final state or federal approval was granted, reported that Alabama Power Vice President Ed Hatch presided over a large meeting in Centre at which he set out to "present facts and figures…concerning the proposed dam at Leesburg." The article said Mr. Hatch reported to the crowd that the project was not yet a certainty. "If Alabama Power builds a dam at Leesburg," Hatch was quoted as saying, "the following are some of the pertinent facts." He went on to say that the area to be permanently flooded by the project was somewhere in the neighborhood of 26,000 acres, according to preliminary surveys conducted by Alabama Power engineers. (The final number turned out to be 30,200 acres.) Of that total, he said the county would lose around 6,000 acres of pastureland, 6,400 acres of corn and 2,600 acres of cotton. "It is the company's policy to flood as little land as possible in meeting the requirements of the Act of Congress and in providing substantially all of the other benefits desirable in a river development program," Hatch said.

Hatch, perhaps addressing a concern raised by someone among those assembled, made it clear that land flooded by the project would not be removed from the county's tax rolls. "To the contrary, the Company would pay ad valorem taxes on these lands based on the price paid by it for them, along with the dams and power plants to be built." Hatch said the obligation by the company would increase the county's tax income "by approximately $200,000." Hatch concluded the meeting by repeating the company line, reminding everyone that the Weiss Dam project would create "large recreational areas" with "opportunities for fishing, wild life and water sports," while also removing "uncertainties as to the development of the river, the stabilization of water levels, creation of adequate industrial water supplies, and provisions for future water transportation" that would make the Coosa River Valley a prime location for new industry.

The Coosa-Alabama River Improvement Association, a Gadsden-based river development organization founded by William Patrick Lay in 1890, released a booklet around the same time that another newspaper used as source material for an article under the headline, "Dream of Coosa-Alabama Development Nears Reality." The article pointed out that the federal government considered the Coosa "one of the 10 most undeveloped American rivers," and predicted that after construction, Alabama Power's new dams would "attract many industries along its 350-mile course." The article stated:

> *The Coosa-Alabama basin, now principally farming country with a population growth substantially below the state average, should see many large industries moving into the area to take advantage of the water transportation and the abundant power to be available from the new dams to be built by Alabama Power.*

Indeed, census figures indicated a decline in Cherokee County's population between 1930 and 1950 (from 20,219 to 17,364) that would take a half century to overcome.

When Alabama Power officials went to the nation's capital in September 1957 to seek permission from the Federal Power Commission to build the Coosa River dams, Pearson, the Manns and others from Cherokee County were sitting on the opposite side of the courtroom. They presented evidence and testimony they hoped would protect their farms and livelihoods from eminent domain foreclosure.

> *It went on for two days, and I thought we had a chance, a very slim chance. But the power company presented the dam as something they felt like they should do before someone else came in and did it, so they presented the dam as a defensive act as well as an offensive act.*

When the FPC approved Alabama Power's request, the CRVLPA lawyers advised their clients to stop throwing good money after bad. They saw that people in Cherokee County who had long enjoyed quiet lives on the farm were about to be swept into the twentieth century whether they liked it or not. When the federal government granted approval to begin construction, the CRVLPA quietly disbanded, and the group's former members braced themselves for a fifty-five-foot wall of water. "There was nothing else we could do when the Federal Power Commission gave its approval," Pearson said. "At that point, the lake was coming."

RAISING THE DEAD

They conducted a study before the water came up and they worked all summer, meticulously uncovering graves. There were about six or eight graves that they uncovered.
—Martha Baker, recalling a series of archaeological digs at a Native American cemetery near Cedar Bluff in 1958

Internal memos from Alabama Power Company archives in Birmingham give some insight into one of the more sensitive aspects of the Weiss Lake project: the raising or relocating of over a dozen cemeteries in Cherokee County set to be inundated by the rising water of the Coosa River. The memos made clear the importance the company placed on doing the job to everyone's satisfaction. Work began as early as 1956, a year before the Federal Energy Commission granted final approval for construction. Alabama Power sent teams of surveyors to locate and catalog every cemetery, whether active, inactive or long abandoned, that might potentially be affected. Next, the company hired three men, Donald Formby, George H. Nason and Ollie Smith, to make contact with church groups or other organizations responsible for the administration and operation of the cemeteries. If cemeteries were inactive or privately owned, the company dealt with the property owner. The most time-consuming phase of the operation, according to one memorandum from June 1960, was locating family members of the deceased in order to acquire permission for relocation.

> *We made every effort to contact every next of kin relation and in some cases where graves were old and relatives were uncertain of their kinship, we obtained permission from almost anyone and everyone by the same name as the deceased, hoping that this would establish an attitude that we were*

leaving no stones unturned to secure proper permission before attempting to relocate any human remains.

According to a study compiled in 2005 by the Northeast Alabama Genealogical Society titled "Cemeteries Impacted by the Weiss Dam and Lake of Cherokee County, Alabama," a total of fifteen cemeteries were relocated or raised above the future lake level, including four cemeteries listed as "unnamed cemetery" numbers one through four. The others were Calcedonia, Cedar Bluff, Clayton, Clifton, Graveyard Hill, Howell, Lawrence, Sand Valley, Smith, Trotter and Wright Cemeteries. Each chapter in the Genealogical Society's book dealt with a specific cemetery and included photographs of the relocated grave sites, along with notations from interviews conducted by Formby, Nason or Smith with at least one relative for each of the deceased. For example, the following notes were compiled for the grave site of Mr. Wash Garner, who was interred in Sand Valley Cemetery:

I talked to B.F. Garner about the marked but unnamed grave No. 147, June 18, 1958. This is according to the survey of the Sand Valley Cemetery, made by Alabama Power Company. He said "Wash Garner is the occupant of grave No. 147." August 28, 1958, I interviewed Mrs. Bessie McGuffy at Gadsden, Ala. She said the occupant of grave No. 147 is her deceased brother, who died in 1892 of diphtheria. She signed a permit allowing us to raise the level of the cemetery.

Other notes compiled by Alabama Power officials and reprinted by the Genealogical Society described various general characteristics of the original cemetery before it was moved or raised. Regarding Calcedonia Cemetery, the entry read as follows:

This is a currently (1959) used cemetery at the Calcedonia Baptist Church. There are a total of 180 graves in the cemetery with 97 being marked and 83 being unmarked. The contact person for the cemetery is J.M. Jones of Route 2, Centre.

The notations are typical of those uncovered by the Genealogical Society. In the notes for Cedar Bluff Cemetery, Alabama Power officials remarked that of 466 marked and 527 unmarked graves, only 100 were within the flood pool and required raising. At the Clayton Cemetery, all 33 graves were moved to another location. The Clifton Cemetery was an inactive cemetery

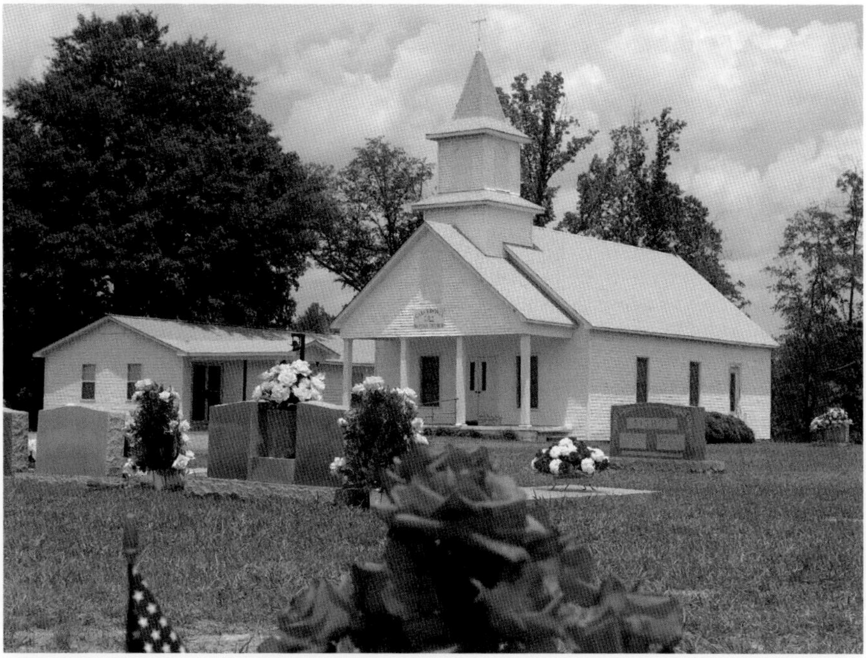

The cemetery at Calcedonia Baptist Church is one of over a dozen that was raised to prevent its inundation by Weiss Lake. *Photo by the author.*

containing 50 grave sites and was left intact because, according to Alabama Power, "the burial plot will be on an island when the water is at flood pool level." Alabama Power also decided against disturbing Graveyard Hill and its 100 unmarked graves because "it will be situated on a three-mile island surrounded by Weiss Lake." All of the 132 graves at Lawrence Cemetery were moved to another cemetery, but only 11 were relocated from Sand Valley; the other 406 were simply raised above flood level.

After all efforts to contact relatives of the deceased were exhausted, the company advertised its intentions in the *Cherokee County Herald*, "after which a 30-day period was allowed before actual relocation was started." When relocation began in January 1959, one memo noted, "the three years spent in preparation were beneficial, because it gave ample time to study the situation. It avoided costly mistakes from a monetary and public opinion standpoint."

Other memoranda from the Alabama Power archives specify the requirements for grave-site relocation, including acquisition of a supply of "painted pine boxes of sufficient sizes to adequately contain organic remains, casket hardware, and all other items found in the original graves."

Monuments and tombstones were photographed and documented before being relocated. Each casket also contained a four-inch by four-inch granite marker, on top of which was engraved a two-inch number that corresponded with a number assigned to each original grave site. A metal plate was nailed to each pine container to aid further in the relocation process. Also, the contract stipulated that the contractor who removed the remains was responsible for furnishing "a spray of artificial flowers with an average retail value of $5 to $7 for each grave relocated."

Alabama Power worked with churches and other organizations to acquire land adjacent to their existing facilities whenever the situation required relocation of the entire cemetery. The company either bought the land and deeded it to the church, or donated to the church or cemetery organization a monetary amount sufficient to allow them to purchase the land. The company also landscaped and seeded new sites after the bodies were reburied. In four cases where cemeteries were partially below the lake's future flood contour, Alabama Power raised all the markers, monuments and other items and used maps and survey crews to duplicate the cemeteries at their new elevations. "This accuracy was necessary because each item had to be replaced, after the filling operation, to sign within one inch of its original relative location," a memo stated. In the April 3, 1960 issue of the *Montgomery Advertiser*, Cherokee County native Bob Ingram wrote a column describing the raising of one cemetery along the banks of the Coosa River, pointing out that the bodies beneath the relocated tombstones "now lie 25 to 35 feet under the ground instead of the customary six feet."

Cemetery operations had been active for over a year when Nason, located in Centre, sent a correspondence to coworker D.D. Hill in Birmingham describing efforts to relocate three cemeteries in the county. Under the subject line "Coosa River, Weiss Dam," Nason wrote:

> *On May 2, 1960 I visited Sand Valley, Cedar Bluff and Calcedonia cemeteries and made a careful inspection. Mr. Formby and the sub-contractor for the tombstones had previously made a careful inspection...I find the cemeteries and tombstones to be in excellent condition.*

Nason also wrote that at Sand Valley and Calcedonia Cemeteries, the affiliated churches had held their annual decoration ceremonies the day before "with large crowds attending each." He said parishioners from both congregations told him they were quite pleased with the company's efforts. In fact, Nason wrote, "both groups seemed to feel that the cemeteries are in much better condition than they were before the work commenced." Nason also informed Mr. Hill that "grass seed and fertilizer have been furnished to responsible parties for seeding of each cemetery." He concluded his memo by suggesting the final payment for moving the graves be paid to Mr. Hugh Steele of Centre "as set out in Paragraph Y of the contract."

Another party responsible for relocating grave sites in Cherokee County was Julius A. Scherwin Jr. of Aiken, South Carolina, who moved 188 graves for the U.S. Army Corps of Engineers. (The Corps was involved in peripheral aspects of the construction project such as determining post-construction flood elevations.) The total paid to Scherwin was $15,665, according to a telegram sent by Smith to Alabama Power headquarters in Birmingham. "The work has all been completed and it was very satisfactory," Smith wrote on May 5, 1960.

> *He worked with a minimum of supervision from us. He had no accidents. We were so well satisfied with his work that we will arrange our future schedules so as to be sure that he will bid on them and if he is anywhere near the low bid, we expect to award the contracts to him.*

In a return letter from Alabama Power a month later, Birmingham-based Houston Cummings wrote back to Smith, informing him that Alabama Power had, as of June 8, 1960, "completed a phase in cemetery relocation, and I feel that at the end of this first year it is very timely and would be well to compile all activities and procedures pertaining thereto and to summarize work done in order to evaluate results."

Smith displayed a sense of humor in a June 13, 1960 letter to Real Estate and Right of Way Superintendent W.E. Coleman of the Appalachian Power Company in Virginia. Apparently, in answer to a request by Coleman for advice on commencement of a similar cemetery-relocation project of his own near Roanoke, Virginia, Smith wrote:

> *I had the boy who has been in charge of cemetery relocation give me a memorandum summarizing what procedures he followed. I find that he is much better at relocating cemeteries than he is at writing memoranda, but for what value it is to you, I am enclosing a copy.*

In the following paragraphs, Smith summarized the company's procedures, but a copy of "the boy's" memorandum could not be located in the company archives.

A third group involved in cemetery relocation work in Cherokee County is mentioned in a memo dated July 26, 1960, from Nason to Smith. The correspondence sought Smith's signature on an attached contract that would pay a company called Griffith & Griffith $1,000 for fill work, removal and resetting of headstones at Howell Cemetery.

Native American Sites

A copy of Alabama Power's monthly magazine *Powergrams* dedicated multiple pages of its December 1959 issue to a series of archaeological digs conducted earlier that summer at sites in Cherokee County. The study, financed through a grant by Alabama Power, was conducted by David L. DeJarnette, the director of Moundville State Park near Tuscaloosa and a member of the faculty at the University of Alabama. Dr. Walter B. Jones, state geologist and director of the Alabama Museum of Natural History, had surveyed the area in 1956 and found over three hundred Indian sites within a fifteen-mile radius of Cedar Bluff. *Powergrams* explained that dozens of sites were initially inspected and were considered worthy of a more comprehensive look if appropriate "signs," such as arrowheads, pottery shards or flint points, were uncovered. The June 1973 issue of the *Journal of Alabama Archaeology* lists over two dozen sites in the Weiss basin that received special attention, including six on the A.H. Trotter property in Yancey's Bend, two at the former site of a ferry on the Coosa River, four in Seven Springs and five on property owned by Haynie Johnson in the Coker Ford area. Any area that "yielded one or more potsherds as well as numerous flint chips and points" was classified as a village site.

The digs were conducted by first marking the entire site to be excavated with small squares, which were then staked and marked with a number. That number corresponded to a bag in which relics collected from the area were placed for safekeeping. "Digging is actually a type of careful scraping operation and is done by levels," the *Powergrams* article explained. "The depth of a level is usually six to eight inches. When one level is finished, the diggers go deeper and continue until 'undisturbed' soil is found." It was in the lower layers of soil that artifacts often waited to be discovered. The *Journal of Alabama Archaeology* reported that DeJarnette and his team uncovered "a great deal of limestone-tempered, fabric-marked wares" at the Yancey's Bend digs, "probably as a result of the influence of nearby Tennessee River Cultures of the period." At the former Bradford's Ferry site, three miles southwest of Cedar Bluff, archaeologists found a dozen Indian burial sites, including one with "the skeleton…on its right side in a partially flexed position." At the Coker Ford excavation, ceramics found in burial mounds indicated that "the people who inhabited the area during the Middle Woodland period were probably related to similar documented natives who lived in Alabama and Tennessee." At the Lanier Cobia site, along the north bank of the Chattooga River near Gaylesville, DeJarnette's team found a burial mound over fifty feet long that proved to be among the "most outstanding features of the…period in this part of the Coosa Valley."

In a photograph from the Bradford's Ferry dig reprinted in *Powergrams*, Dr. Jones sat knee-deep in a test pit, where he and members of DeJarnette's crew used "trowels, grapefruit knives and small brushes" to unearth Native American grave sites. In many cases, artifacts were estimated to be thousands of years old. The article noted that archaeological digs in the Coosa River area usually turned up the former sites of Indian villages. Burial mounds were seldom discovered, so the unearthing of two mounds at the Little River site was particularly interesting. DeJarnette noted that not all Indian mounds were burial mounds because Native Americans also constructed temple and effigy mounds. However, like the Cobia site mound, the mound near Little River contained human remains and was "built by lining graves with stones, then heaping large boulders, found in the river and earth, on top." DeJarnette explained that such practice was typical of the Woodland period, "some 2,000 years ago."

Cedar Bluff resident Martha Baker, whose husband Bob owned the "old Haney-Johnston property" where the Little River dig was conducted, remembered the site and what she saw during a tour one summer afternoon:

> *There was an old Indian village off by the side of Little River. It had once been a very large village. The University of Alabama conducted a study before the water came up and they worked all summer, meticulously uncovering graves. There were about six or eight graves that they uncovered. There was one grave with a female and a young child inside, and she had her arms folded over the baby. It was very, very interesting.*

DeJarnette told *Powergrams* the burial customs of the Creeks and Cherokees varied through the years. "Usually they dug one grave, put in the body, and perhaps located several other graves in the same vicinity. Then they began the mound building, piling up of earth over the graves." DeJarnette said that as other family members died, their graves would be placed in the mound, usually in a round-shaped fashion. "The type of burial most frequently used was that of the body flexed. This was the burial custom of some Indians at a later period."

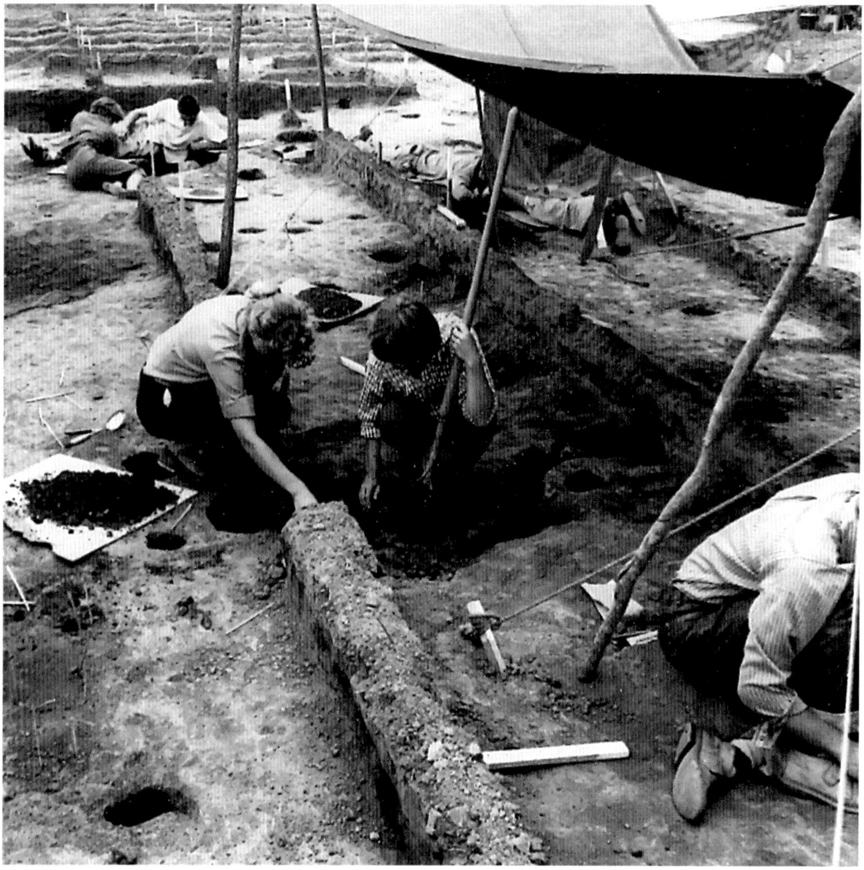

Archaeologists from the University of Alabama conducted digs at various locations in Cherokee County during the summers of 1958 and '59. *Courtesy of the University of Alabama Museums.*

DeJarnette said determining the age of relics and artifacts unearthed in the grave sites involved several factors, including designs on the objects and, in the case of skeletons, studying the bones and skulls. The article noted that graves and relics found at the sites around Cedar Bluff were estimated to date back at least two millennia. On several occasions, diggers unearthed glass beads, wine bottles or pieces of iron that enabled the archaeological team to estimate when various Native American tribes in the Coosa River area had made contact with Europeans. "Scientists can trace the dates of manufacture of many articles which, by certain characteristics, indicate the European country in which they were manufactured." The article also mentioned the newly discovered method of carbon dating, which is used to

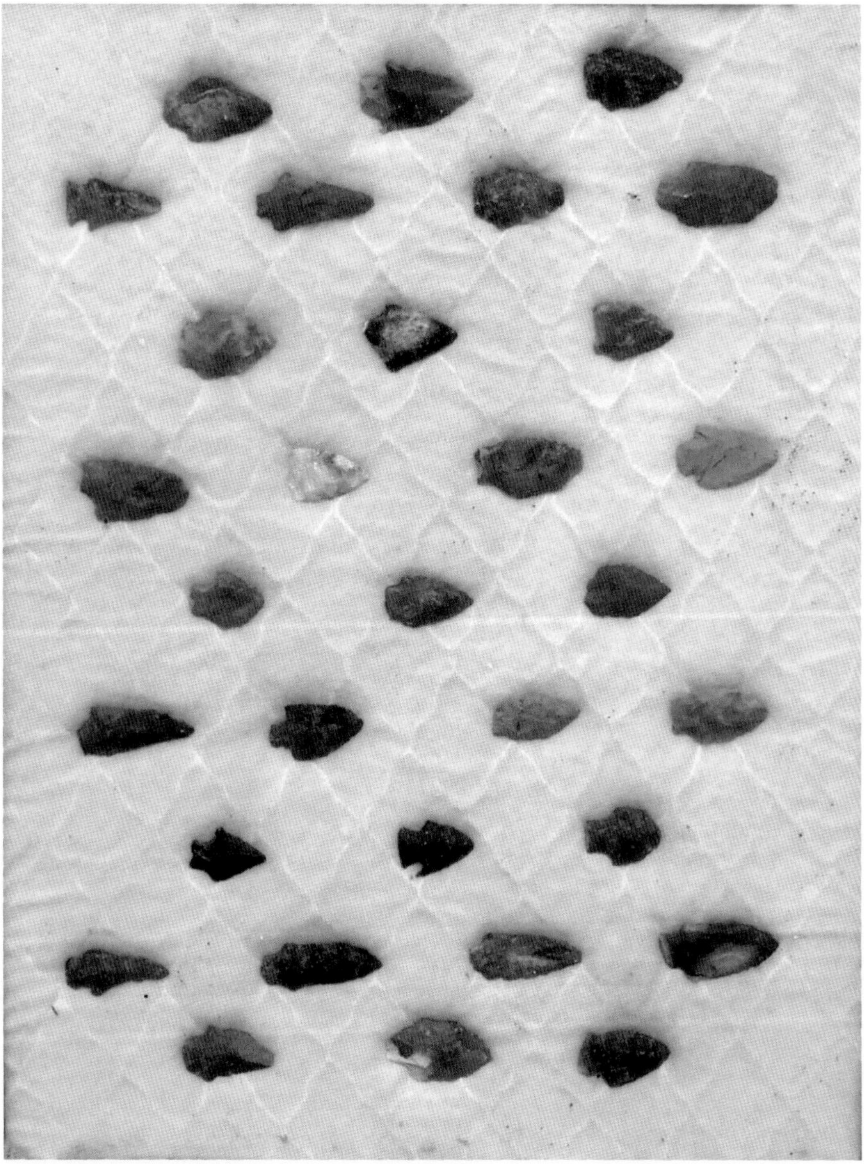

Arrowhead hunting has been a popular pastime in Cherokee County since long before Weiss Lake was built. These framed pieces are part of a private collection, whose owner asked to remain anonymous. *Photo by the author.*

determine the age of objects such as skeletons, shells, charcoal and other organic material.

Just as the people of Cherokee County did in the decades leading up to the construction of Weiss Dam, the Coosa River Valley's original inhabitants occasionally had to deal with Mother Nature. According to the *Powergrams* article, two test pits revealed post molds, a sign that the Creeks who once lived there raised their houses off the ground in order to keep clear of the springtime floods. "You could also see where the stilts had been buried in the ground that they used to hold up their houses," Baker remembered. "I guess they had to build them that way because the water would come up so fast." DeJarnette described the Indians' homes as having vertically stacked logs, daubed together with mud and covered with thatched roofs.

In a report of the early history of the upper Coosa River area prepared for Alabama Power in 2000 by Kleinschmidt, a Virginia-based energy and water resource consultant firm, additional information compiled in the 1980s helped shed more light on the extended history of the Weiss Lake area. The report, based on information from around 320 archaeological sites located inside the Weiss project lands, estimated that settlements in the Weiss area were virtually abandoned by the mid-seventeenth century, probably due to European epidemic diseases initially spread by explorers in the second half of the 1500s. Nearly two hundred years later, whatever remained of the original population had migrated to present-day Childersburg, Alabama, clearing the path for other wayward Indian tribes to settle the Weiss basin. "Manifestations of Native American cultures after 1750 are not well known for the Coosa Valley," the report stated. "During the eighteenth century, the Cherokees moved into the Weiss Basin area in response to growing pressures induced by European-American settlers." Unfortunately, unlike the cultures that preceded them, the Cherokees weren't in the northeast Alabama area long enough to leave behind much of anything besides a few arrowheads and their name.

As they dug into the ground for evidence of the inhabitants who preceded the Cherokees, Jones and DeJarnette worked quietly with delicate strokes and measured movements to expose precious pieces of Native American history. In dozens of other locations around the county, crews with implements much more obtrusive than brushes and trowels would soon begin a different type of earth-moving project with historical implications of its own.

CLEARING THE WAY

When they were burning the brush piles, it got so smoky at the house that you couldn't breathe at night, or anywhere in Cherokee County.
—James L. Wright

The job of clearing a large swath of the thirty thousand acres that would eventually become Weiss Lake began in earnest in the summer of 1958, in dozens of places all over the county, all at once. Julia Wright was eight years old when the first massive Euclid earthmover she had ever seen came blasting over the hill at the family home near Mud Creek in the Osceola community, roaring, whining and spouting smoke. The big green machine scared her so badly that she ran into the house and hid. James L. Wright was in the front yard with his younger sister that morning. He was thirteen years old when the "Euc" came barreling down County Road 22, and he remembered what happened next:

> *It went past the house, just flying, and I reckon it got down to the bottom of Barnes Hill and the driver realized there was nowhere down there to park. So he turned around and drove back up to our house and parked in the front yard. It sat there for a few days until they got started working, and just about everyone in the community came by to take a look at it because no one had ever seen anything that big before. There were cars parked in our yard all the time, the whole time it was sitting there. The tires must have been six feet tall.*

It took months to clear the acres and acres of trees from the Mud Creek area, and before the job was finished Wright was old enough to actually work

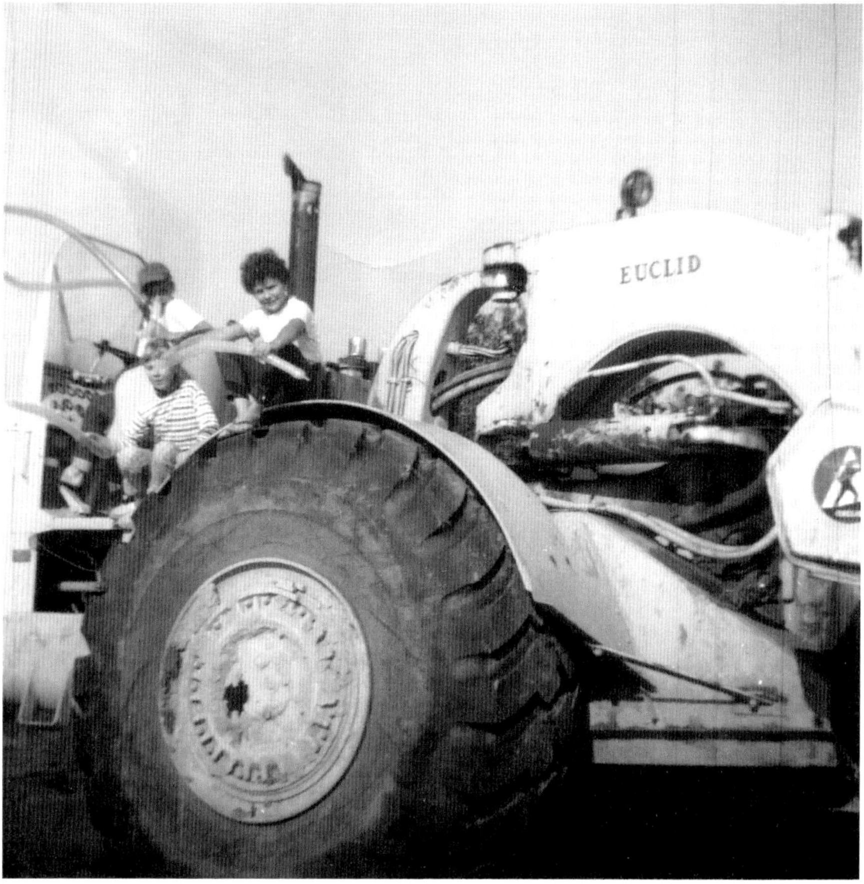

Julia Wright (right) poses on a gigantic Euclid earthmover, which sat parked in her front yard prior to the beginning of construction of the causeway over Mud Creek, circa 1958. She is joined by her brother, Neil Wright, and first cousin, Susan Wright. *Courtesy of Julia Coheley.*

as a member of the construction crew responsible for clearing the murky, muddy bottoms. He also helped build a new, raised causeway connecting Osceola with Kirk's Grove, the community on the other side of the creek.

> *It took them two years to build that causeway, and I did drive a sheep-foot roller behind a big Ford tractor for Bates Construction Company. We were too young to do a lot until right at the end. I got paid sixty-five cents an hour. That was a lot of money back then.*

Wright said construction crews began the clearing process sometime in 1958 by mowing down all the big trees in the Mud Creek bottoms with

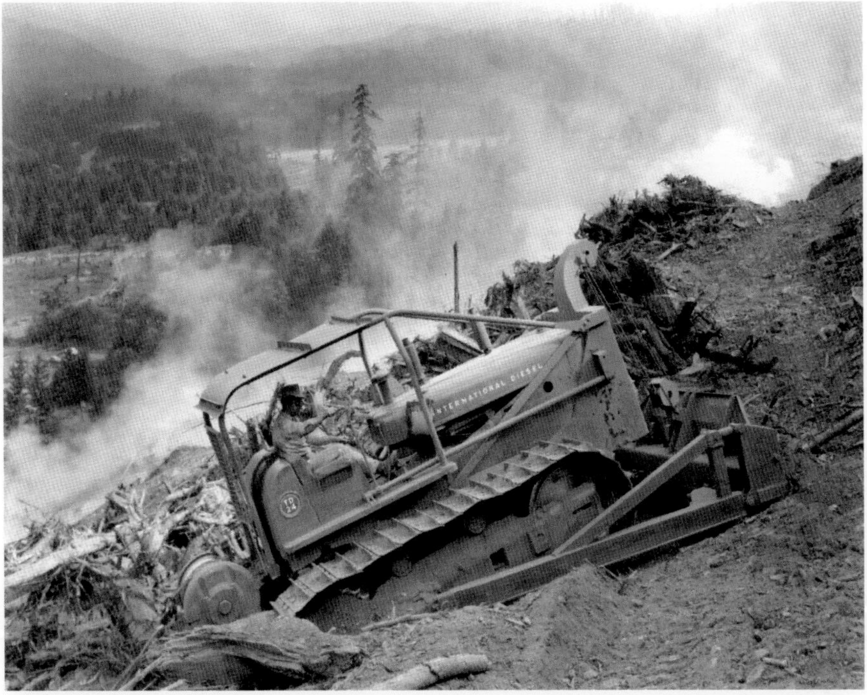

International TD-24 bulldozers similar to this one plowed through forested areas around the Coosa River for over two years, felling acres of trees every day to make way for Weiss Lake. *Courtesy of the Wisconsin Historical Society.*

International bulldozers. "They had those TD-24s with huge blades, and could chop down trees as big around as truck tires." He said there were usually smaller pieces of mechanized equipment moving in a line behind the larger tractors.

> *There'd be little three dozers—and they weren't small, but that other one was a giant—running along behind it so that if it got stuck in the mud or something, the other three could pull it out and get it going again. It cut down everything and kept going.*

Next, the TD-24s lined up beside each other and pushed the fallen timber into massive piles to be burned. Afterward, crewmen—as many as fifty at a time—began the process of walking shoulder to shoulder across the mostly cleared land, whacking through the remaining scrub brush with steel-bladed weed trimmers. "Those were the first hand-held weed trimmers I'd ever seen," Wright said.

> *They'd walk across in a line chopping down anything over three-eights of an inch. Finally, the big bulldozers came along behind them and raked up the trees and limbs and brush for burning. They'd line up five or ten of those TD-24s and they'd pile all that stuff up as far as they could go. Then, they'd go around to the other side and push everything the other way. They would make a pile higher than the trees and several hundred yards long. Then they'd pull up two big gas trucks and spray diesel fuel all over it and set the whole pile on fire.*

He said that for two solid years, the air was constantly filled with smoke:

> *When they were burning the brush piles, it got so smoky at the house that you couldn't breathe at night, or anywhere in Cherokee County. If there wasn't any wind blowing that smoke would just settle across the land, and there'd be a hundred brush piles burning. And they were big brush piles, bigger than a football field. They'd send five bulldozers to repack those brush piles every day.*

George Coheley grew up a few miles down the road from Mud Creek and remembered the bulldozers, the smoke and the months it took to turn the creek bottoms into land suitable for a lakebed. "Those tractors were just amazing," he said.

> *Those TD-24s had blades that went out about sixteen feet in front and the bottoms of the blades lay on the ground. They'd just take it like cutting a field, and they'd have three or four of them in a row and take out a big strip of trees with every pass. Those trees just fell every which way.*

Coheley said he even saw construction workers use mule teams and heavy cables to remove hand-felled logs from low-lying areas too swampy for the dozers. All in all, he said, the clearing process was a truly remarkable event. "We'd never seen anything like that around here," he said. "And it went on for a couple of years."

While tons of heavy equipment were out in the bottoms knocking over trees and piling brush, high-powered attorneys were hard at work attempting to complete a different type of clearing project. By most accounts, Alabama Power Company and the attorneys who represented it in Cherokee County dealt fairly with the people who stood to lose their farms or homes, or both, to the lake. A promotional publication written in the early 1960s for distribution to schools, chambers of commerce and local libraries boasted that "during the more than 50 years of Alabama Power Company's existence it has won a reputation for forward thinking and fair dealing." In another newsletter, the company claimed that "90 per cent of all the land it has acquired for its numerous projects has been by mutual agreement" and considered the number proof that landowners generally considered it to be reasonable when it came to land purchases. "The company's appraisers are familiar with land values and appreciate that every acre of land in an area does not have an identical value. Waste land is not worth as much as highly productive crop land and other lands are worth something in between." Alabama Power promised that each parcel would be considered individually and that "no one need sell until an agreement has been reached on a fair price or until disinterested third parties determine the fair price and it is determined by the court."

Still, the legal section of the February 18, 1959 edition of the *Cherokee County Herald* was filled with page after page of condemnation notices. Alabama Power was listed as the plaintiff in a civil action against J.T. Webb and others for "3,625 acres, more or less, of land in Cherokee County, Alabama." The announcement, to Webb and other unlisted owners, read in part:

> *You are hereby notified that Alabama Power Company, a corporation, has filed its written application in this Court, seeking to condemn the lands therein described for the construction, maintenance and operation of Weiss Dam, the main reservoir; the diversion dam or navigation facilities connected therewith, or for works appurtenant or accessory thereto…*

The listing documented dozens of individual tracts ranging in size from less than one acre to nearly four hundred acres, all or some of which "will be completely submerged by the proposed Weiss Dam reservoir when it is filled to its normal elevation of 564 feet above mean sea level." The listing ran to over three full pages before the next one began; then came the next notice and then the next.

Gary Mobbs was the son of a sharecropper who farmed in Yancey's Bend near Cedar Bluff before the lake came. He said the landowner whose property his family farmed made accommodations that allowed the Mobbs clan to continue making a living on another farm. But he said other families had to find alternative sources of income, and for that reason he insisted most people would have been better off if the river had been left alone:

> *Some people will tell you the lake was the worst thing that's ever happened to Cherokee County and I'm one of them. People used to have a place to make*

a living. Now there's nothing here. Everybody has to go somewhere else to make a living. Mr. A.H. Trotter saw that we had a place to go, so it didn't affect us. But other people had to get jobs in Georgia or somewhere else. It was like a plant shutting down, and they had to go. All the sharecroppers just had to do the best they could. I know a few got rich off the land, but a lot didn't. That's my personal opinion.

Bobby Joe Johnson, a lifelong resident of the county who played football at Jacksonville State University before spending most of his career as a teacher and coach at Cherokee County High School, was in college when Alabama Power first began sending lawyers and appraisers into the area. He remembered that some people weren't treated as fairly as he thought they should have been. Johnson's father owned property along the riverbank near the Tate's Chapel community in Centre. "We got $103 an acre for our property, and the further away you got from the dam, the less they'd offer you," he said. "I remember that some people up around Alexis only got around seventy-something dollars an acre." He stopped short of claiming that the simple farming community got taken advantage of by Alabama Power and its legal team. But just barely:

I don't think they realized—the people who had the good farmland—that the lake was going to take all of it. If you decided you didn't want to sell and wanted to fight it, they just condemned it and went ahead and backed the lake up, anyway. You had no say-so. They'd still pay for it, eventually, but only after it went through the courts. Of course, we were all ignorant about it. There was one attorney in Cherokee County at that time who knew about this stuff and could have helped people, but that was Hugh Reed and Alabama Power hired him to work for them.

Johnson said that despite his best efforts to acquire federal funds for a series of locks, the county's representative in the United States Congress was ultimately unable to keep his promises to the people who sent him to Washington:

Albert Rains was our congressman and he thought [the lake] *was really going to be a boon for this place. Of course, he got fooled, too. It just didn't work out that way. He told the people that thousands were going to come in here, that there would be new industry coming in and navigation locks that would open the river from Rome to Mobile. But it never happened. It's just been in the last twenty years that people have really started to come in here.*

Newspaper articles from the time exude the same enthusiasm Johnson and others often heard from elected officials. A special advertising section from the *Cherokee County Herald* in early 1957 beneath the headline "Cherokee Expecting Big Industrial Boom" made progress on a colossal scale sound inevitable. One of Alabama Power's new dams, it read, "will be located near Leesburg and will provide Cherokee County with some of the South's choice industrial sites" because "hydroelectric dams will assure prospective industries plenty of power" and "the river, when developed, will provide good transportation."

"Big things are expected of Cherokee County!" read the headline of a two-page advertisement purchased by the city of Centre in the same special section of the *Herald*. The ad continued:

> *Cherokee County's leaders are looking forward to another very progressive year. The future of this county, and area, is tied closely to plans for development of the Coosa River. Cherokee County is not waiting until this development becomes a reality; already, preparations are being made for a time when river navigation and additional hydroelectric power, combined with plenty of commercial water, will attract new industry and thousands of tourists to Cherokee County. Leaders of the county believe this area is on the threshold of the most progressive era of its history.*

Johnson's uncle, ninety-three-year-old William Johnson, another lifelong resident of Cherokee County, said he never believed the story about the locks and was never keen on selling out to the power company. But he realized pretty quickly that there was nothing he could do to stop construction of the lake, so he grudgingly took what was offered. Ultimately, he admitted, he ended up on the good side of the deal:

> *I got $121 an acre. Different people got different prices. I held out for two years, and then got a registered letter in the mail telling me my money was in the Cherokee County Bank. They came in here and had every lawyer hired to work for them. You can't fight a company as big as Alabama Power. Of course, I made money by the lake. I've sold twenty-five or thirty* [waterfront] *lots.*

Billy Godfrey, a lifelong resident of the Alexis community, was a landowner who insisted he and his neighbors received fair treatment from the power company. "We didn't have any farmland that we lost, but we had some that ended up in the easement," he said.

My mother sold seven acres to the power company for three hundred dollars, because they paid about twenty percent of the value on property in the easement. I told her to ask them for five hundred, but when they offered her three hundred she took it. On the other land, you could bargain with them.

Godfrey said landowners were instructed to pay for an estimate from a licensed appraiser, then get additional appraisals from two neighbors who were not members of the immediate family. Godfrey said a neighbor of his in the Alexis community, Robert Tidwell, asked him to appraise his property:

He said, "Whatever you do, there won't be any hard feelings, just do it the way you think is fair." So I came by with a clipboard and I walked over his place. I went down there and went all the way around his house and he had a well, and a well pump, and fruit trees. And you had to appraise all that, at whatever value you thought it had. I appraised it all, the house and everything. He also had some swamp land and I didn't value that too high, but he had six acres out here on the road and boy, that's high. He said I was pretty good because I got within two dollars of the appraiser he had hired. If I remember right, I appraised everything he had for $9,100. That may not sound like a lot today, but back then you could build a good house for about $5,000. Things were cheap back then.

Godfrey said he supposed Alabama Power representatives wanted estimates from someone other than an out-of-town appraiser in the interest of fairness. "And I think most people got a fair deal from them," he said. "The only people who were against the lake were the ones who were going to lose all their land. For some of them, that land had a sentimental value. You could have given them a million dollars and they wouldn't have been satisfied."

OLD HOUSES, NEW HOMES

Houses can be destroyed, but memories will remain.
—Frances Underwood, Gadsden Times *staff writer, 1958*

It only cost $412, Louise Nelson said with a smile. Originally known as Snow Hill after the family that built it in 1870, the home occupied by Robert and Louise Nelson once sat on what is now an island in the middle of Weiss Lake. "We lived in Rome, Georgia, and Alabama Power had put the house up for bid," Mr. Nelson said. "I put in a little old bid of, what was it Louise?"

"Four hundred and twelve dollars," she answered.

"Yeah, that's what we paid for the house," he smiled. "Then we paid $6,000 to have it moved."

Mrs. Nelson said the house was little more than a shell when they went to inspect it after the purchase, "and vandals had broken in and destroyed the staircase and knocked out a lot of the windows."

Mr. Nelson said when he bought the house he really had not thought about moving it. He figured maybe the house could be torn down and the lumber used to build another house, where he and his wife could raise their family. "One day he called me from his work and told me, 'Well, we've bought the house.' And I said, 'We did? What are we going to do with it?'" So Mrs. Nelson's father, Paul McWhorter, gave them forty acres in the middle of the hundreds he owned. Shortly thereafter, Mr. Nelson set about finding someone to move the house from its location in Yancey's Bend to where it sits today on County Road 92.

"I talked with three house movers and the first two said they wouldn't touch it," Mr. Nelson recalled. "Finally the third man, his name was I.L.

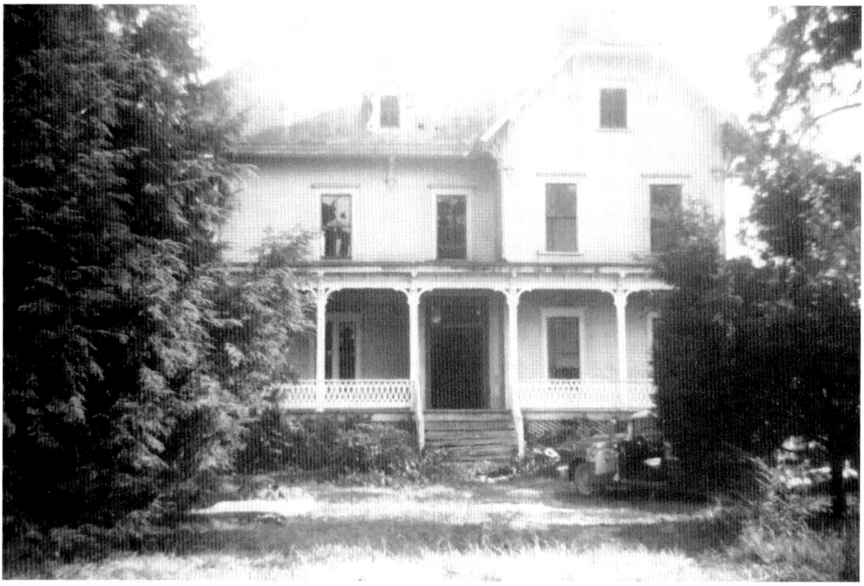

The house once known as Snow Hill originally sat near the end of Sewell's Ferry Road. *Courtesy of Robert and Louise Nelson.*

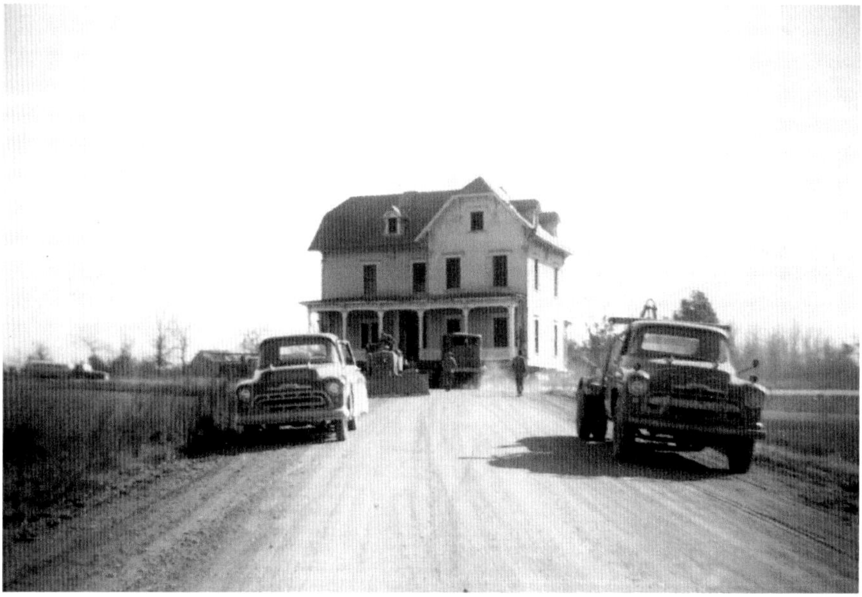

The Nelsons bought the former Snow Hill for $412. They paid $6,000 to have it moved several miles northeast of Yancey's Bend. *Courtesy of Robert and Louise Nelson.*

Davis, said he'd move it for us." The Nelsons said the move involved two semi-trucks, a dozen axles, steel I-beams and a lot of planning and patience. "Mr. Davis had to make sure both drivers, the one in the front and the one behind the house, turned their steering wheels at exactly the same time on every curve," Mrs. Nelson said. "It was like watching someone conduct an orchestra." Nelson said there was one obstacle in particular that Davis and his employees had to maneuver around in order to move the house. "There was a little, narrow bridge up the road just a little bit and there was no way to get the house over that bridge," he said. "So he had to cross a little creek bed to get it past the bridge."

Anxious to get the house relocated, Mrs. Nelson said she called her father on the day the operation was scheduled to begin. "I wanted to be down here for the move but I had small children so I called my dad to see how the move was going," she said. "He told me he'd go down and check on the progress, but he never called back that night. The next morning I called him again and asked if they'd started the move. He said, 'Yes, Louise, but I'm afraid they've taken the wheels out from under it and gone home, and the house is sitting in the middle of a creek.'" Mrs. Nelson said she quickly gathered

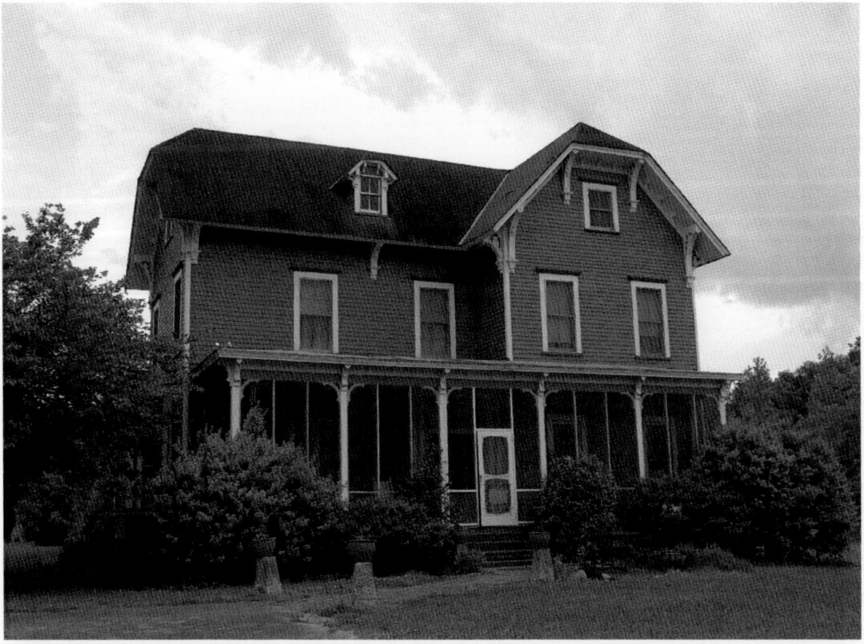

Today, the remodeled home of Robert and Louise Nelson sits on County Road 92 near Cornwall Furnace. *Photo by the author.*

the kids and rushed from Rome to Cedar Bluff. "By the time we got there, they already had the house out of the creek and back on the road. My father hadn't been able to see the wheels because they were under water. He just assumed they'd had a problem and left it there."

From there, the drive up Highway 9 and onto County Road 92 was relatively uneventful. After building a foundation and setting the house down, the Nelsons and their children moved in, even though the interior was far from finished. "We got the kids' rooms ready and then we slept in what was the dining room, until our bedroom was finished," Mrs. Nelson recalled. A little over two years later, on the day President Kennedy was shot in Dallas, Mr. Nelson said he was helping a group of men install the red oak flooring he bought to cover the original pine.

"I sure remember what I was doing that day," he said.

The Lawrence Home

"The ways of progress can be ruthless," began the article by Frances Underwood in the *Gadsden Times* in 1957. "This could be the thoughts of Mr. and Mrs. Sam Lawrence as they prepare to move from the home inherited from their ancestors." The article recalled how the second-story balcony of the large colonial house, which sat near the current site of the boat ramp on the Highway 9 causeway between Cedar Bluff and Centre, was once a respite for Civil War soldiers. Sam Lawrence was a farmer who worked over 160 acres of cattle, cotton, corn and hay. His father, John Lawrence, had completed the home in 1867 after buying the property from the Watt and Wester families in 1859. Sam Lawrence's wife, the former Mary Medlock of Gaylesville, painted china and spun her own draperies and bedspreads on an old-fashioned loom "set up in one of the back rooms on the first floor of the eight-room house."

Construction of the house started before the War Between the States broke out but was not completed until shortly after the fighting ended. Sam Lawrence said in the article that all the lumber for the house "came off the land, which had to be cleared, and the massive oaks were hewn and planed into logs when this house was constructed." All the floors in the house were made of the same hand-dressed lumber. "It is recalled that much of the beautiful furniture now in the home was hidden under straw in the attic of the house," the article said. "This furniture was not found by the destructive Yankees, but saved to grace the home after the war was over." The house, along with a stone milk house and a barn built in 1876 with sixty-foot logs held together with pegs and bolts, was torn down and burned to make way for the lake and the new raised highway.

Peggy Pearson, whose husband, Forrest, was one of the founders of the Coosa River Valley Land Protective Association, said she remembered the beautiful white columns of the Lawrence home and the reaction Sam and "Miss Mary" had to their forced eviction: "They left and never came back," Pearson said. "They said they just couldn't stand to see their farm and old home place underwater. So they moved to Auburn and never came back."

The Towers Home

Newspapers from the mid-1950s are filled with stories of antebellum homes that sat in the way of Alabama Power's plans for Cherokee County. In 1958, *Gadsden Times* staff writer James W. Smith Jr. gave the account of a "rambling, two-story home with its large fireplaces" that was built at a time when a steamboat port near Leesburg called Turkey Red was a stop along the route between Rome and Gadsden. The Towers home was built using rock hauled by oxen from Lookout Mountain and timber felled and finished on the property. George Washington Towers built the home on land originally homesteaded by President Grover Cleveland to Francis M. Davis, who sold the property to Towers in 1895. Towers established a trading center on the site, where he also "operated a mercantile store, cobblers shop, gin, grist mill and flower mill." The home was built for his wife, the former Bertha Mayfield Lowe, and it soon "became the 'stopover' point for commercial travelers. At the Towers home, the welcome mat was always out." After Towers died, his wife continued to operate the facilities he had built over the years.

Eventually, one of the Towers girls married J.H. Miller, and it was they and their children who lived in the house when the article appeared in the *Times*. "The food freezer has replaced, to a great degree, the smokehouse, with its rows of hams and shelves filled with canned vegetables and fruits," the article noted. But despite the addition of "electricity and other modern conveniences" the Millers "still use the two large fireplaces." Smith also wrote that the Towers grandchildren and great-grandchildren "have been busy the past several weeks preserving the shrubs and bulbs planted more than sixty years ago by Grandmother Towers. Several truckloads of these plants have been moved to the home's new site, some two hundred yards from where it now stands."

THE RICHARDSON-BISHOP HOME

The two-story, white-columned house that today serves as a business office in Centre has been moved twice since it was completed in 1862. Originally located in Yancey's Bend near Cedar Bluff, the old Richardson-Bishop home was constructed using "some of Cherokee County's finest virgin, long leaf pines," according to a story by Dixie Miller in the September 12, 1962 issue of the *Anniston Star*. When Alabama Power backed up the Coosa in 1961, most of Yancey's Bend ended up beneath twenty feet of water. Lafayette M. "Faith" Bishop, the overseer of the Yancey plantation after the end of the Civil War, built the house for his family but rented it out for a short time before moving in. Bishop married the former Martha Daniel and the couple eventually raised fifteen children in the house. Tragedy struck the Bishop

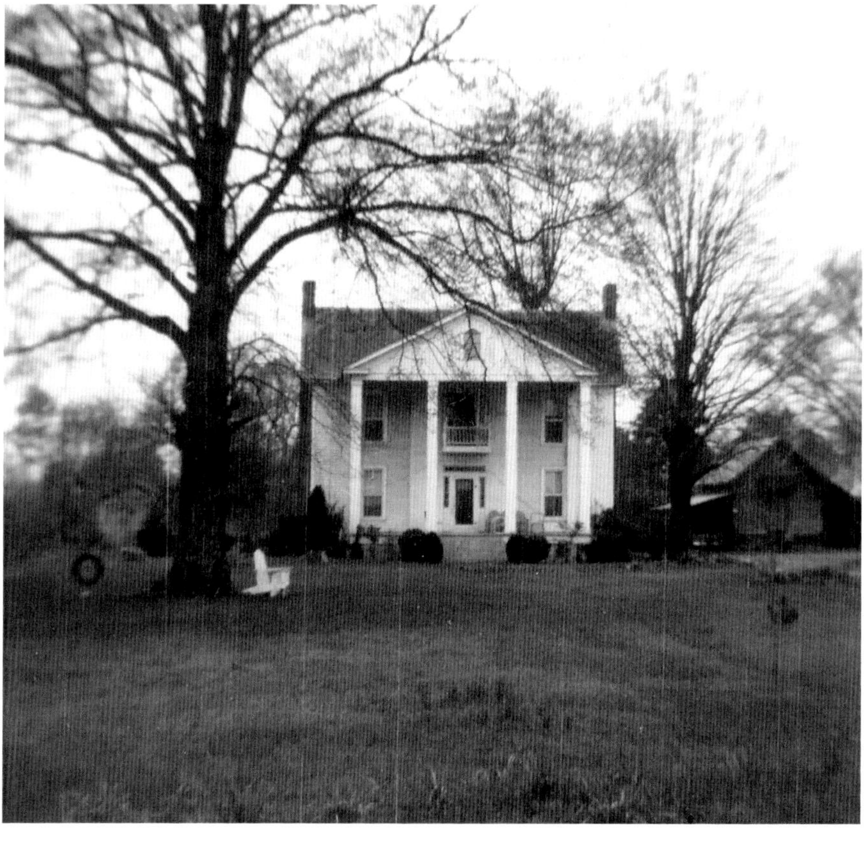

The Richardson-Bishop home, completed in 1862, at its original location in Yancey's Bend near Cedar Bluff. *Courtesy of the Cherokee County Public Library.*

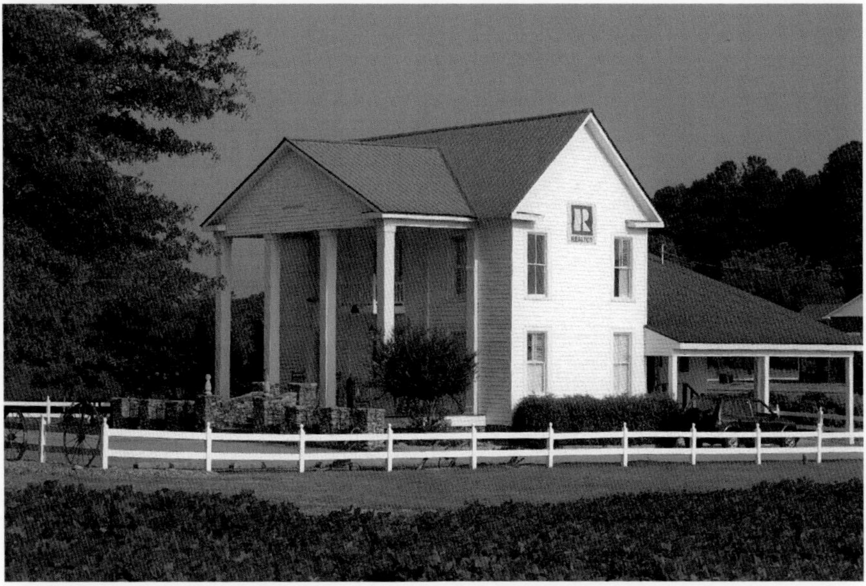

The Bishop house was moved in the late 1950s to make way for Weiss Lake. In 1997, new owner Shad Ellis had the house moved again, to Centre, where today it serves as his business office. *Photo by the author.*

clan several times over the years, including the loss of a two-year-old girl, who drowned when she fell headfirst into a half-full can of lard, and two young boys who were killed when a shed they had sought shelter in was blown over during a sudden thunderstorm. After it changed hands several times beginning in 1919, the family home was bought by Sarah Richardson in 1954. When Alabama Power received final approval from the federal government to begin the Weiss Dam project in 1957, Richardson told Miller she wanted to make sure the house was saved.

The current owner of the home, Shad Ellis, continued the story from there:

> *Bert Cobia moved the house from Yancey's Bend to where it sat for forty years alongside Highway 9 near the end of the four-lane in Cedar Bluff. There weren't any power lines then, just cotton fields, so he pulled it straight there. When they got it moved, they upgraded to the pine paneling we have now and added a bathroom. They also added back one of the two original fireplaces. When I bought it and moved it here in 1997, we tore off the old bathroom and added another.*

Round Mountain

If the forced relocation of an entire family from their homestead was an unsettling possibility in Cherokee County, then the hundreds of people who lived in the Round Mountain community in the late 1950s must have been downright heartbroken. Located in the northwestern center of the county, Round Mountain had the sad misfortune of being named after a rise it surrounded but did not occupy. The farming and milling hotspot was positioned at the base of the tiny bump near the southern end of the Appalachians, directly in the path of the soon-to-be-rising waters of the Weiss reservoir. In a story in the *Gadsden Times* titled "Round Mountain to become 'lost town,'" Dixie Miller discovered one of the more poignant aspects of progress in northeast Alabama.

> *There will only be nostalgic memories of the social life that centered around the clubhouse, of the boy who galloped five miles on his horse to bring a doctor and help save a young girl's life, or of a barefoot, 9-year-old boy who walked the dusty road of the mining quarters peddling milk.*

In her article, Miller explained that Round Mountain began in 1835, "when some settlers stopped, built cabins and grubbed out a few patches of row-crop land." The exact date was not recorded in history, but the locals recalled the story thanks to generations of retellings handed down through the community. The first recorded history of Round Mountain came from the early 1840s, when William Milner settled in the area and built a forge "to shoe oxen and mules and to repair ox carts and wagons." Surely the stories of settlement years earlier must be true, Miller reasoned, since otherwise there would have been no wobbly wagons or bare-hoofed beasts of burden.

The Round Mountain Furnace was in operation by 1852, built by a man named Moses Stroupe, a native of Lincoln County, North Carolina. The pig iron forged at the furnace was shipped out on steamboats headed for Rome. After the operation was purchased by Captain J.M. Elliott, production was "boosted to 12 tons a day" to supply materials for the Rebels during the Civil War. "But the Yankee soldiers destroyed the furnace," Miller wrote. After the war, Elliott rebuilt the furnace and formed the Round Mountain Coal and Iron Company in 1871. Soon, he was turning out twenty-five tons of pig iron a day, some of which was shipped to Pittsburgh and used to make "car wheels and rolls for rolling mills."

Round Mountain grew larger still a short time later, following the establishment of the Round Mountain Wood and Alcohol plant, which was managed by Henry Shackleford, a man Miller identified ominously only as "from the North." As settlers began to drift into the community to search for employment in the mills and factories, dirt roads were carved into the soil, and homes sprung up along their edges. For decades, a covered wooden bridge spanned the Chattooga River and connected Round Mountain to Cedar Bluff. A man named John Baker "helped haul lumber from the R.B. Kyle Lumber Mill at Cornwall to build the beautiful clubhouse, considered then a majestic building with eight rooms on the first floor and two huge rooms upstairs." The second-floor rooms, used mainly for boarders and social gatherings, were brightly painted, Miller wrote, with windows that stretched from floor to ceiling and a side porch that "led off from the big kitchen which had a huge fireplace." By the late 1880s, railroad lines connected Round Mountain to Rome, Attalla, Decatur and points beyond, and the Tennessee-Alabama-Georgia Railroad laid a spur to a new freight facility the company had recently erected a quarter mile from the furnace. The iron stored at the depot, Miller wrote, "was shipped to Gadsden and used until the age of steel."

Miller's well-researched story ran to several thousand words and explained how a little boy sold his milk to the miners living on the "working" side of town; how young Jack Fox galloped thirty minutes each way to bring a doctor from Cedar Bluff who saved Sue Brandon, his classmate at the Round Mountain schoolhouse, from a "congested chill"; and how, in 1907, Roy Chancellor's horse saw something coming up the road that "looked like a buggy but there was no horse hitched to it." The first "motor buggy" to pass through Round Mountain belonged to Charlie Ward Sr. of Centre, Miller explained. A year later, the community was introduced to another "contraption," the telephone.

Sadly, as the twentieth century began to seep into Round Mountain, the nineteenth century was leaving just as fast and taking a huge portion of the local population with it. The furnace failed in 1907, and the wood and alcohol plant closed in 1912. The railroads pulled up their spur lines in 1917, and by 1933 the once-treasured clubhouse had changed owners several times and was "beginning to 'go down.'" The student population at the local schoolhouse was consolidated with Cedar Bluff in 1944, thus completing the community's demise. Miller concluded her article by asking her interviewees about future plans. One elderly woman had already moved into a house beside her daughter in Centre. Two others were still looking for new homes. Miller wrote that they and many other lifelong residents of Round Mountain "still don't know where they will go" after the Coosa River swallowed their community.

In *Rivers of History*, Professor Harvey Jackson wrote that settlers to north Alabama in the early 1800s often noted in letters to friends and family that the Coosa "curved to touch every farm in the valley." For over a hundred years, the swishing, swirling waters of the river had been a blessing to people fortunate enough to live within a few minutes' walk of its banks. Decades later, the same would be true again. But to the hundreds of families who lost homes, farms or even entire communities to the dust, smoke and noise of Alabama Power's $30 million construction project, proximity to lowlands along the riverbank must have seemed like a curse.

FROM START TO FINISH

It was rough. They'd call you in the middle of the night if they needed you.
—Kenny Gossett, apprentice pipe fitter on the Weiss Dam construction site in 1958

Not long after Alabama Power Company Chairman of the Board Thomas W. Martin announced the letting of contracts to build Weiss Dam in June 1958, construction began near Leesburg. The initial $9.5 million contract, won by Morrison-Knudsen, Inc. and Moss-Thornton Co. mandated that work be conducted simultaneously at the spillway and powerhouse sites in order to have the dam's hydroelectric generation facilities online by June 1961. According to former Moss-Thornton vice president of engineering Charles H. "Hack" Sain, his firm had worked with Morrison-Knudsen on a pair of earlier construction projects and decided to split duties on their newest contract:

> *Moss-Thornton worked on the steam plant at Wilsonville, Alabama, and Morrison-Knudsen worked at Leesburg. It was just a joint venture, but M-K was the sponsor of the dam so they ran the show. The only time Moss-Thornton had anything to do with Weiss was when M-K would call and ask us to help them out. We furnished some equipment, but that was about it. That dam would have been more than Moss-Thornton could have handled, and M-K was definitely a heavyweight in the construction business at that time.*

By July 31, 1958, Morrison-Knudsen crews had relocated to Cherokee County from other construction sites around the country and joined a group of local workers. Together, they began the process of erecting the

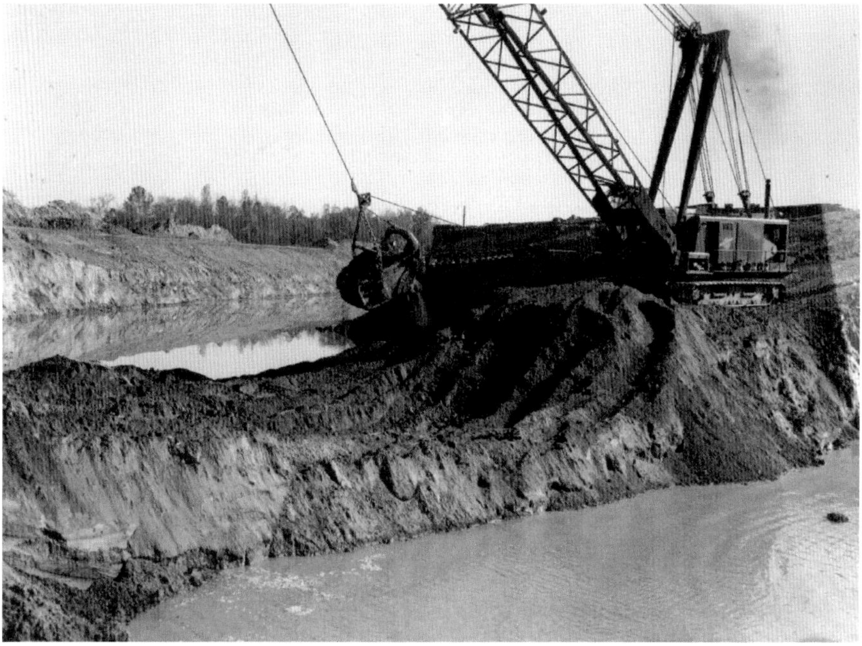

Construction crews used draglines to dig a diversion channel for the Coosa River before beginning construction of the spillway dam. *Courtesy of Alabama Power Company.*

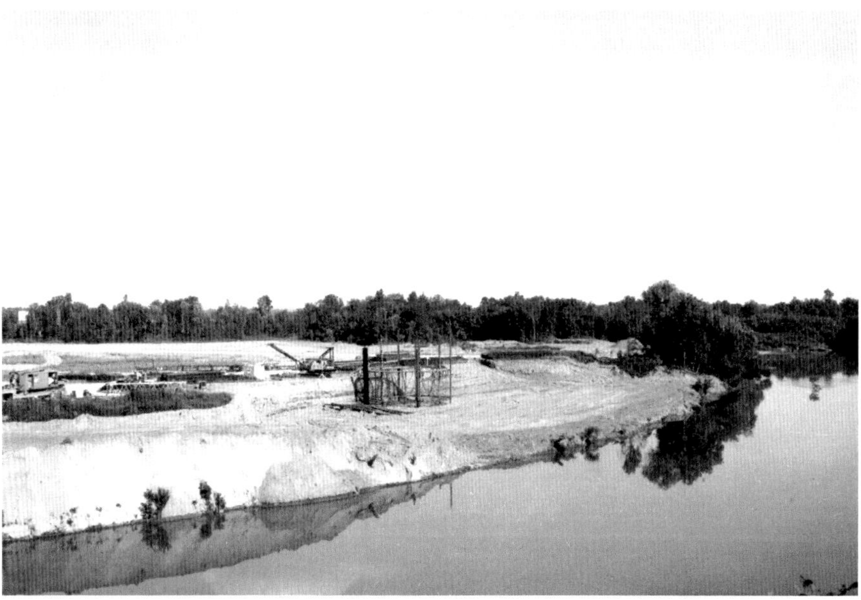

The steel shell used to build individual cells of the cofferdam sits on the bank of the Coosa River. *Courtesy of Alabama Power Company.*

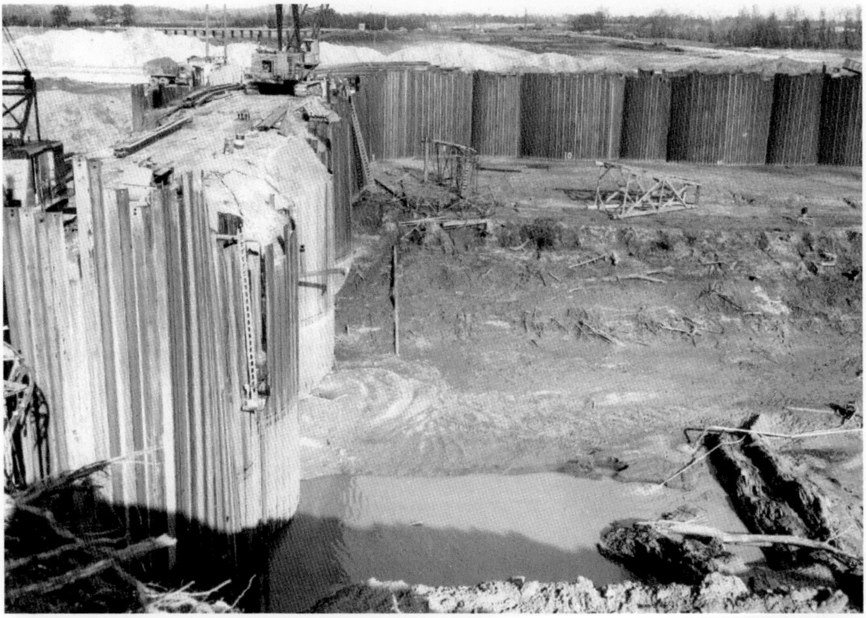

After the cells were pounded into bedrock and filled with waste materials, the riverbed was pumped dry to create the construction site for the spillway. *Courtesy of Alabama Power Company.*

humongous cofferdam at the spillway site. By mid-October, according to articles in the *Cherokee County Herald* and *Coosa River News*, a temporary diversion canal had been excavated with draglines. Simultaneously, other crews were constructing a watertight enclosure in the main river channel using temporary metal cells, which were interconnected to form the cofferdam.

Each of the twenty cells composing the cofferdam enclosure was sixty feet across, made up of 16-inch-wide, 60-foot-long steel strips. Crane operators used a 135-foot boom to hoist the individual steel strips into place around a moveable metal skeleton. After the strips were interconnected to form a hollow shell, the crane swung the cylinders into place in the riverbed. Crews then used massive pile drivers to pound the frames into bedrock before filling them with clay and waste materials. Subsequent cells overlapped, eventually creating a rectangle of several acres across the Coosa, which was pumped dry to form the construction site for the spillway, or diversion, dam. Centre native Kenny Gossett was a nineteen-year-old apprentice pipe fitter on the Weiss Dam project in 1958, and he remembered seeing the cofferdam crawl its way across the river:

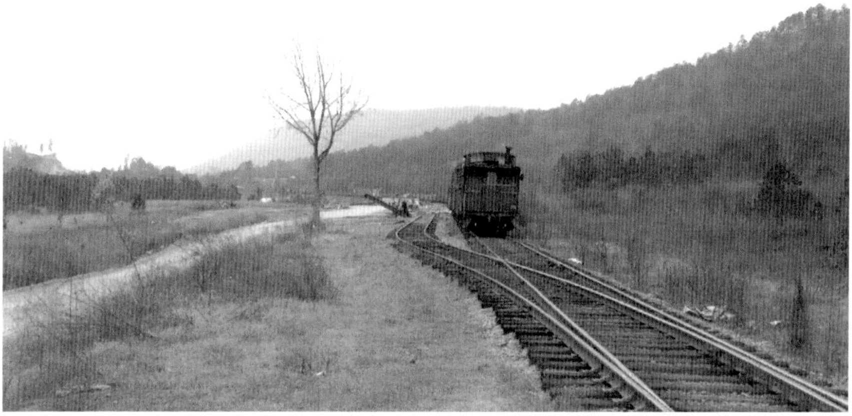

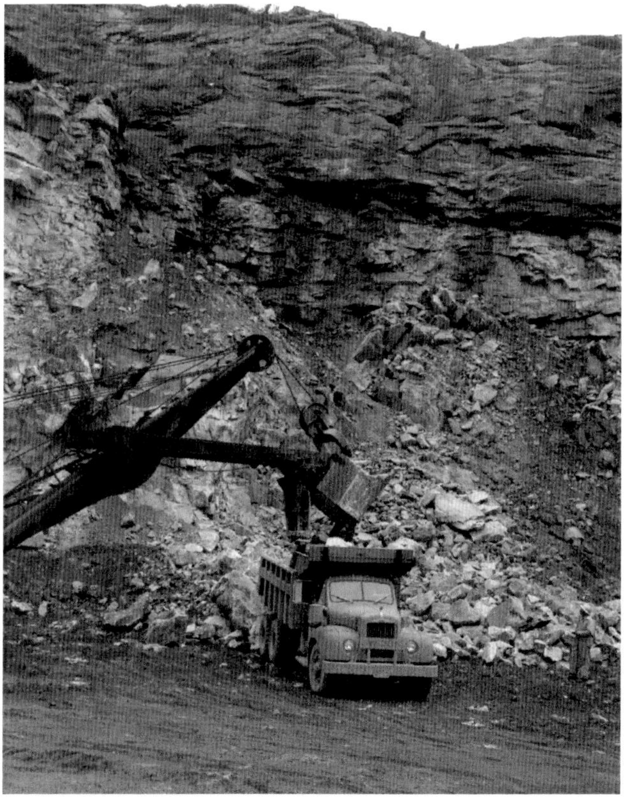

Above: Cement was brought in via the railway spur line near Ewing. It was then hauled by truck to the batch plant near the spillway and used to make concrete. *Courtesy of Alabama Power Company.*

Left: A sandstone quarry near Leesburg provided the aggregate used to make concrete at the batch plant. *Courtesy of Alabama Power Company.*

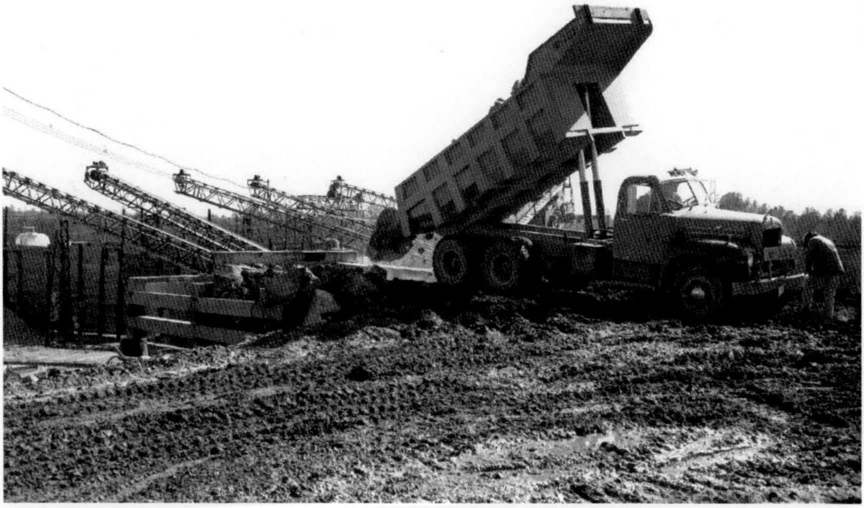

Rock hauled by dump trucks from the sandstone quarry was crushed into various sizes of gravel and even sand. *Courtesy of Alabama Power Company.*

> *They'd use those interlocking metal pieces to make the round cofferdams. Then, they'd fill each one full of dirt so they could cross it and start on the next cell. They went all the way across the river doing that.*

Near the spillway site, Morrison-Knudsen erected a mobile concrete mixing plant previously used at the company's Table Rock Dam site in Missouri. A 120-foot-tall lighting tower at the spillway site held aloft forty thousand-watt floodlights, which allowed the M-K crews to work round-the-clock in order to try and meet the scheduled completion date. For the next several months, day-shift workers stayed busy building concrete forms and placing them for the night crews, who poured concrete from four-cubic-yard buckets suspended over the spillway site and brought into position by the huge boom crane. Company documents indicate the total amount of concrete used for the 460-foot-long, 90-foot-tall spillway was 59,000 cubic yards; another 83,000 cubic yards was used to construct the powerhouse. The total amount of reinforcing steel was 3,650 tons.

Excavations at the powerhouse site determined how deep crews would have to dig to reach bedrock. Workers then used bucket rigs to remove large rocks and dig drainage channels to expose the bedrock and keep the worksite as dry as possible. All of the concrete for the spillway and powerhouse was mixed on-site at the batch plant near the cofferdam. Rocks were hauled by truck from a sandstone quarry near Leesburg and dumped onto a conveyor belt at the plant, which emptied into large hoppers that separated, cleaned, crushed and sorted the fragments into various sizes and textures. In a story printed October 18, 1958, and subtitled "Leesburg's Landscape Changing," M-K Office Manager Fred Bader told a reporter for the *Gadsden Times* that summer rains had delayed the project, but that the "cofferdam cells are 70 per cent finished; the site for the powerhouse is cleared, and the quarry is almost ready to go into operation." The ten-thousand-foot-long shortcut that would eventually chop a twenty-mile stretch out of the Coosa and connect the spillway to the powerhouse was on track, as well, the reporter noted: "Some of the world's largest earth moving equipment is being used now to create the beginning of the canal." Work at the powerhouse site had already progressed to the point that "the bedrock is exposed in a large area."

According to an article in the Alabama Power magazine *Powergrams*, the first concrete was poured at the spillway site on January 29, 1959. The article said cement used to make concrete at the batch plant was hauled

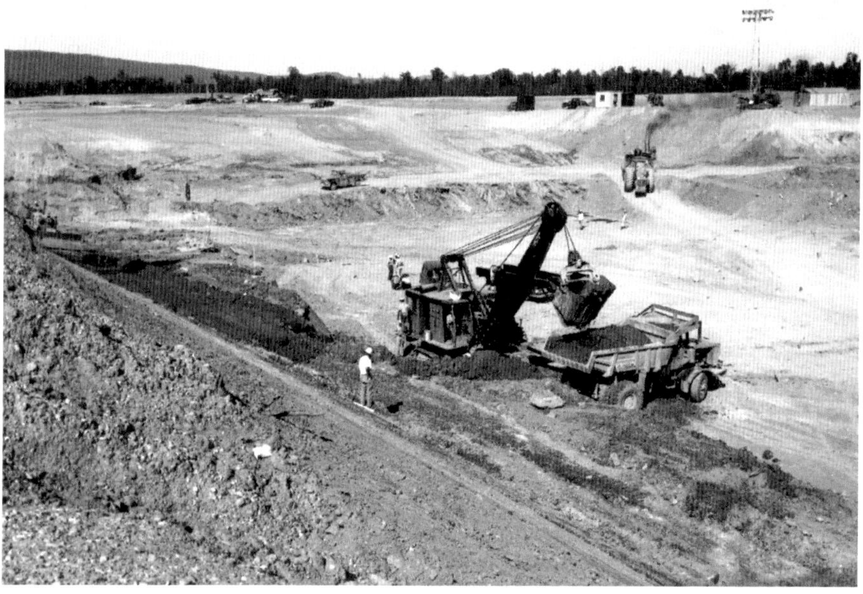

Early excavation at the powerhouse site, four miles southwest of the spillway, required crews to dig down to bedrock before concrete pouring could begin. *Courtesy of Alabama Power Company.*

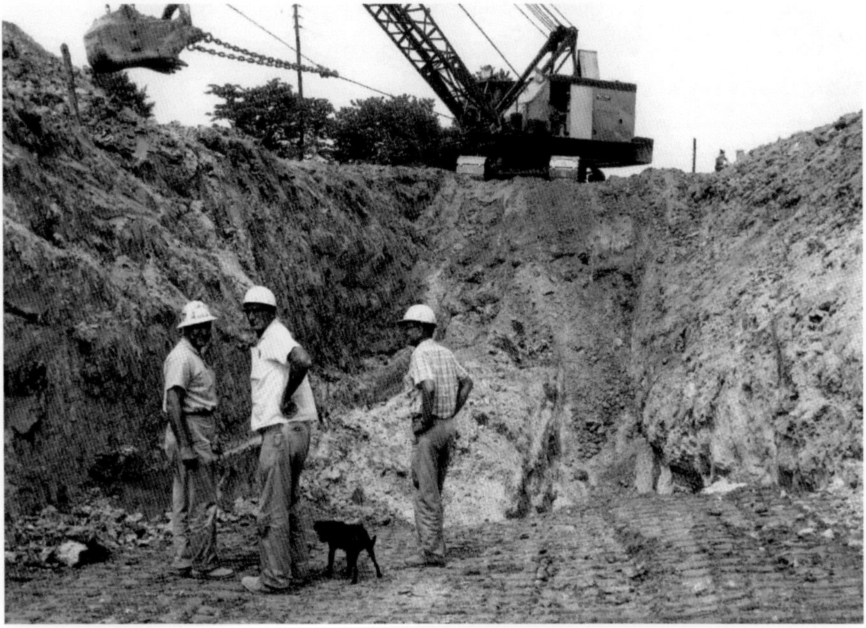

A trio of construction workers and their mascot inspect a trench near the powerhouse construction site on June 18, 1959. *Courtesy of Alabama Power Company.*

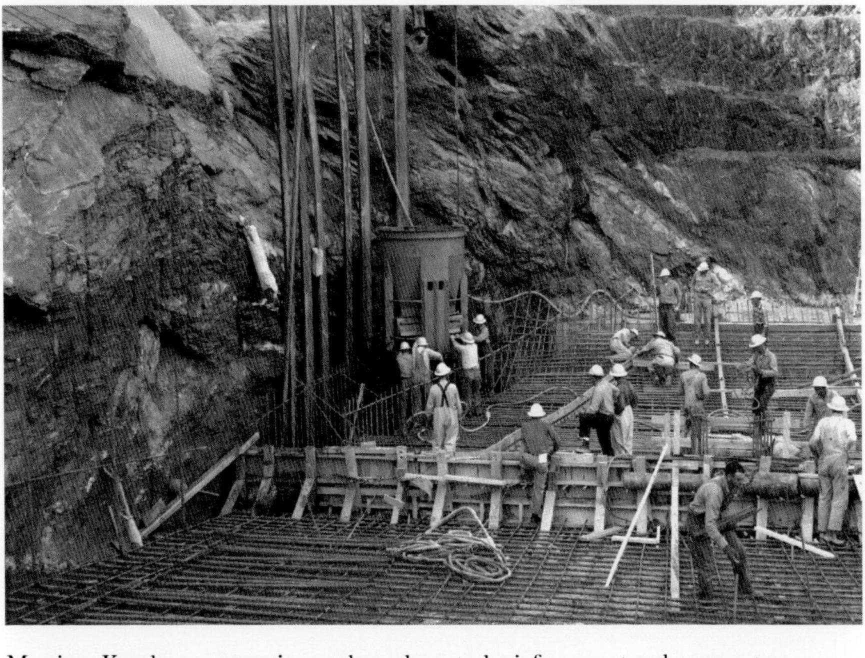

Morrison-Knudsen construction workers place steel reinforcement and prepare to pour concrete at the powerhouse on February 17, 1959. *Courtesy of Alabama Power Company.*

via covered railway cars from a railhead located a couple of miles west of Leesburg, at Ewing, then by trucks to the mixing plant. In a first for Alabama Power, fly ash shipped from the company's Gorgas Steam Plant was used as an ingredient in the concrete mixture. The fly ash reduced costs by limiting the amount of cement required to make concrete and "provide[d] a higher ultimate strength, greater water tightness, reduced shrinkage and improved workability and durability." According to *Powergrams*, all the water used to make the concrete for Weiss Dam was pumped directly from the Coosa.

Morrison-Knudsen was also responsible for the concrete portion of the powerhouse, four miles south-southwest of the spillway. Concrete mixed at the batch plant was transported overland in four-cubic-yard buckets via lowboy semi-trucks to the powerhouse, where another crane lifted the buckets into position for pouring. After each five-foot-thick pour dried, workers raised the wooden frames another five feet, then repeated the process. In a story about the dam that appeared in the weekly newspaper *The Post* in 1999, Gossett explained that if the concrete was poured more than five feet at a time, it would get too hot as it dried and cause imperfections. The potential for overheated concrete was also the reason pouring operations were usually conducted at night.

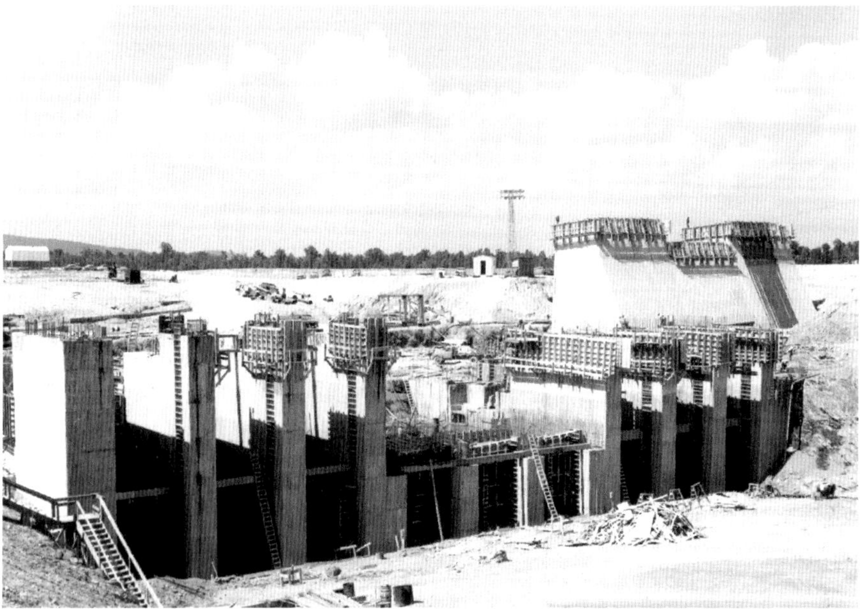

By July 1959, the powerhouse outlet piers, located on the tailrace side of the structure, were beginning to take shape. *Courtesy of Alabama Power Company.*

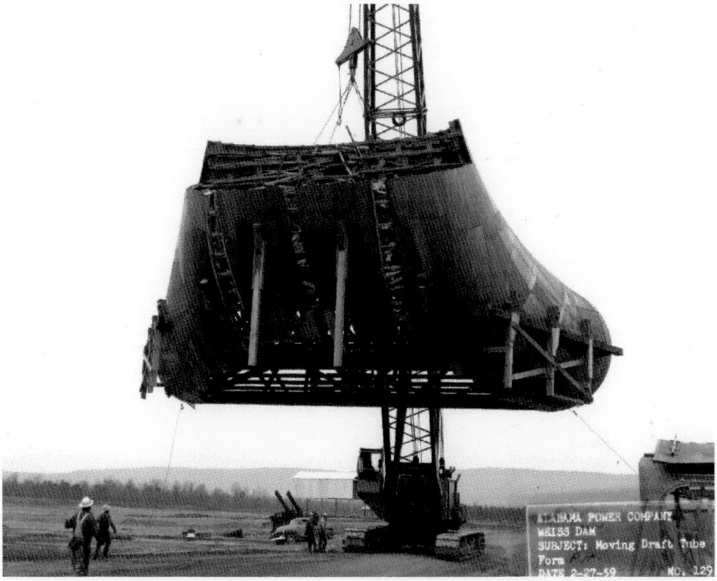

The wood-frame and plywood draft tube form is hauled into place in early 1959. The form was used to shape the outlets that dump the Coosa River into the tailrace after it passes through the turbines. *Courtesy of Alabama Power Company.*

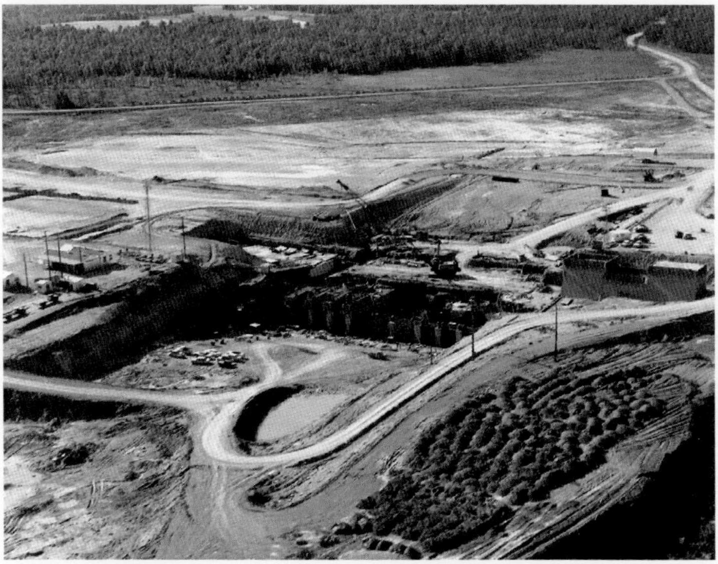

An aerial view of the powerhouse construction site in mid-1959 shows significant progress. The roadway at the bottom of the photo was eventually removed to allow completion of the tailrace. *Courtesy of the Gadsden Public Library.*

Photos from the April 1959 issue of Morrison-Knudsen's internal monthly magazine, *The Em-Kayan*, documented significant progress at the powerhouse site. The massive concrete foundation for the draft tubes was formed and ready for pouring. The wood-frame and plywood form, seen in another photo swinging from a crane like a giant U-shaped vacuum attachment, would be used three times to shape the concrete that would funnel the rushing waters of the Coosa back into the river channel after it exited the turbines. "By last month the job was in full swing on all fronts," read *The Em-Kayan*. "Powerhouse and spillway excavation was virtually completed and concrete placement had begun." Also, the earth-moving phase of the project was on schedule:

> *More than 60 percent of the dikes have been "based in"—in other words, raised from out of soft ground in low areas, thus opening the way for full-scale placement of fill atop long reaches of the dike this summer.*

The article noted that at the height of the operation the construction crew consisted of 350 men directed by project manager Harold I. Maxwell. Other supervisors included project engineer William McDaniel, office manager Fred Bader, concrete superintendent Frank Stevens, carpenter superintendent Al Higgins and excavation superintendent John Logan. C.B. McCullar was listed as the superintendent of construction for Alabama Power.

Leesburg resident Robert Adderhold was a maintenance worker on the dam construction site responsible for keeping dozens of pieces of enormous earth-moving equipment running twenty-four hours a day. He remembered long hours on the job site during his thirty-eight months as an employee of Morrison-Knudsen:

> *I worked two shifts, first and second, because they didn't have anyone else who could diagnose the new equipment that Caterpillar had. They had Euclid and Clarke earthmovers, too, but these were Caterpillar 631's, and they were brand-new. They had electric and hydraulic transmissions and they gave a lot of trouble. I worked out in the field all the time. It seemed like something was always broken.*

On June 3, 1959, alongside a news capsule announcing that eighty contestants were entered to compete for the title at the next evening's annual bathing beauty contest at Centre City Park, a photograph on the front page of the *Herald* updated readers on the progress of Weiss Dam. The aerial photo

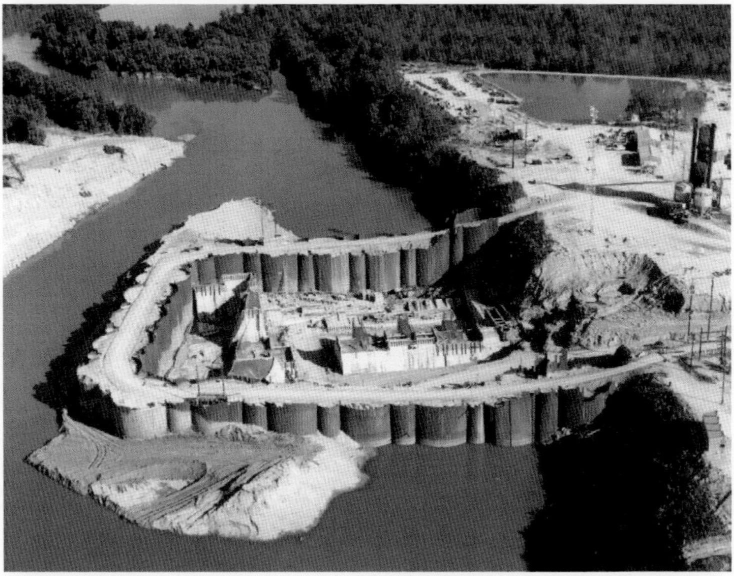

The spillway rises inside the cofferdam. The water flowing around the left side of the construction site has been rerouted into the temporary diversion channel. *Courtesy of the Gadsden Public Library.*

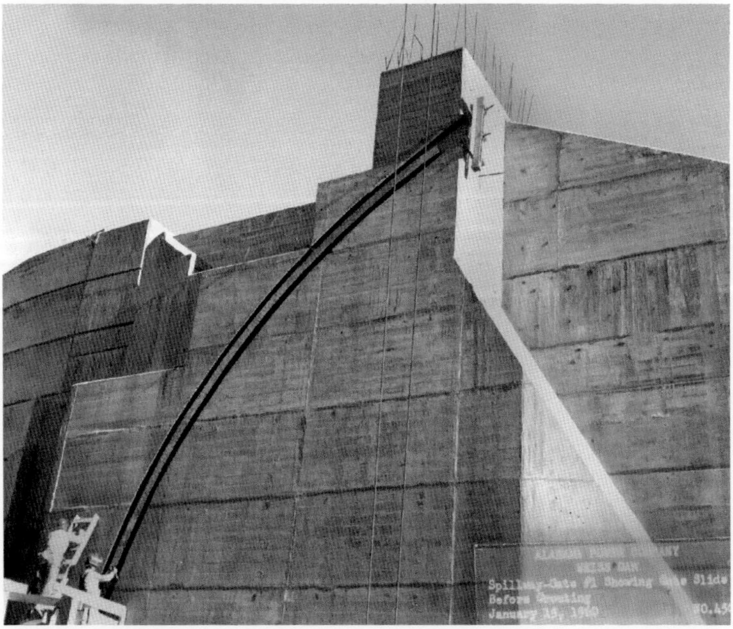

By early 1960, concrete pouring was complete at the spillway. In this photo, workers install slides that guide forty-foot metal gates used to impede the river's flow. *Courtesy of Alabama Power Company.*

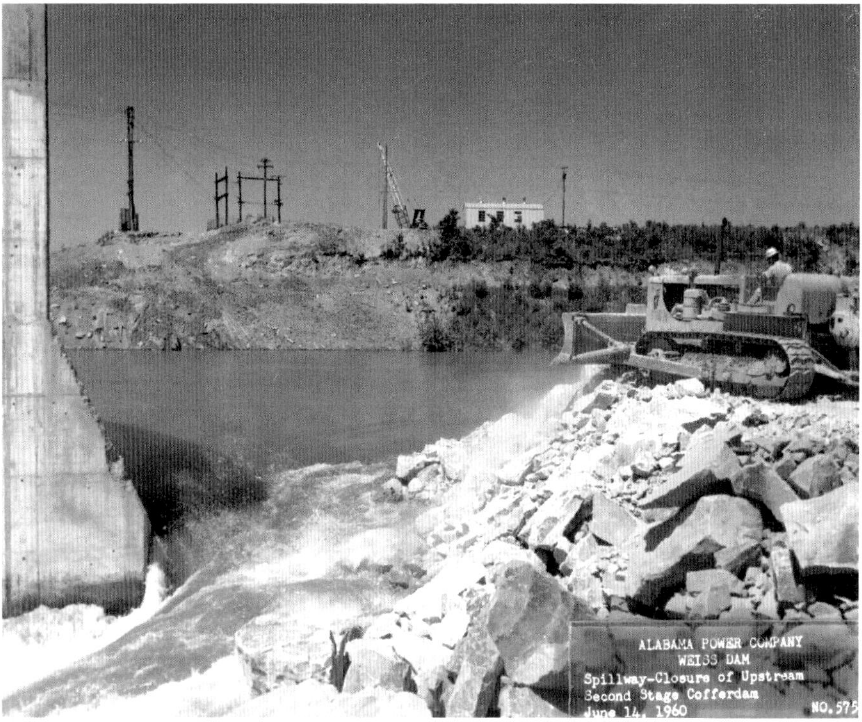

The diversion channel around the spillway cofferdam was closed off in June 1960. *Courtesy of Alabama Power Company.*

showed the spillway rising inside the cofferdam, the Coosa River temporarily redirected around the structure on the Highway 411 side. The spillway piers were almost completed and would be by midsummer. Around the same time, at the powerhouse, the base had already risen forty feet from the bedrock, and pouring of the concrete overflow section was progressing. Swimming pool–sized stay rings used to support each of the twenty-eight-thousand-kilowatt turbines were already in place within the powerhouse superstructure. "By early last month," the article noted, "the MK-MT builders had their job better than two-thirds finished and were expecting to complete work next spring." A schematic from the Alabama Power archives revealed how construction crews condensed the dam into sections, each five feet high, which were colored in with pencil after completion. On-site engineers used the charts to document construction progress and adhere to Alabama Power's tight schedule. By the end of 1959, work was proceeding as planned, and most of the concrete pours on the schematic had been marked off the list.

Aerial photographs from the November 1959 issue of *The Em-Kayan* showed two long, partially completed dikes snaking away from the powerhouse structure as it rose from the middle of a cotton field near Leesburg. The entire facility was surrounded by cranes and dozens of other construction vehicles. Trees in the foreground lined the Coosa River as it zigzagged toward Gadsden. In another photo, enormous Euclid earthmovers, "among the biggest ever employed by Morrison-Knudsen," were lined up for a "noon-hour servicing" of the "nineteen thousand feet" of diversion dikes. A caption beneath the photo explained that the team, made up of eight machines each capable of hauling forty-eight cubic yards of dirt, typically placed as much as forty-seven thousand cubic yards of fill on the fast-rising dikes during two ten-hour shifts. Morrison-Knudsen also had on-site three U.S. Army M-4 tanks stripped of military hardware. Excavation crews used them to pull rolling sheep-foot earth compactors and push the earthmovers.

Before he took a position operating pumps to keep the ground inside the cofferdam dry from the constantly seeping Coosa River, Gossett's job was removing rock from the quarry and loading it for transport to the concrete plant. "I started at the quarry where they drilled holes into the rock to blast for the gravel," he said. "They'd bring in the big rocks from the quarry and run them down a conveyor belt and into the hoppers where they'd grind it up to make whatever size gravel they needed—they even made their own sand." When he moved over to the cofferdam pumps, Gossett said it was keeping the interior as dry as possible that was the most trying part of his job:

> *We had 150-horsepower pumps hanging on the sides, and they were running all the time. But we'd also have to bring big, four-inch pumps in and set them up, run a hose into the deepest of the pools of water, and run that hose over the side and pump the water out of the cofferdam and back into the river, to keep it dry enough so that the men inside there could work on the dam. It was rough. They'd call you in the middle of the night if they needed you.*

In the spring of 1960, Representative Albert Rains was at it again. In a front-page editorial in the May 25 issue of the *Herald*, he again tried to convince the people of Cherokee County—and possibly himself—that there would be a navigable river channel "from Rome to the Gulf of Mexico." Following the approval a few weeks earlier of $200,000 for construction of a dam at Miller's Ferry on the Alabama River, Rains concluded that "at the proper time locks will be installed in the dams on the Coosa River which are being built by the Alabama Power Company." The next week, in a follow-up column, Rains repeated the claim: "When the Alabama Power Company has completed the construction of the five hydro-electric dams on the Coosa River, locks are to be installed by the government, thus making the waterway navigable for 286 miles." Based on the appropriation, which he had received from the House Appropriations Committee, Rains could not resist one more self-administered pat on the back:

> *During the past eight years, despite countless efforts by myself and other members of the Alabama Congressional Delegation, we were not able to get any more money for the Alabama River—until last week. Commitment to Miller's Ferry will ultimately result in Government construction of these projects.*

By June 1960, bulldozers began shoving rocks into the diverted Coosa as crews worked to pull away the steel cofferdam from around the spillway. A few days later, with the enclosure removed, the Coosa once again flowed freely down its original channel, though Alabama Power engineers now had the option of stemming the flow by lowering retractable, forty- by forty-foot steel gates that could be rotated at the push of a button. "The signal

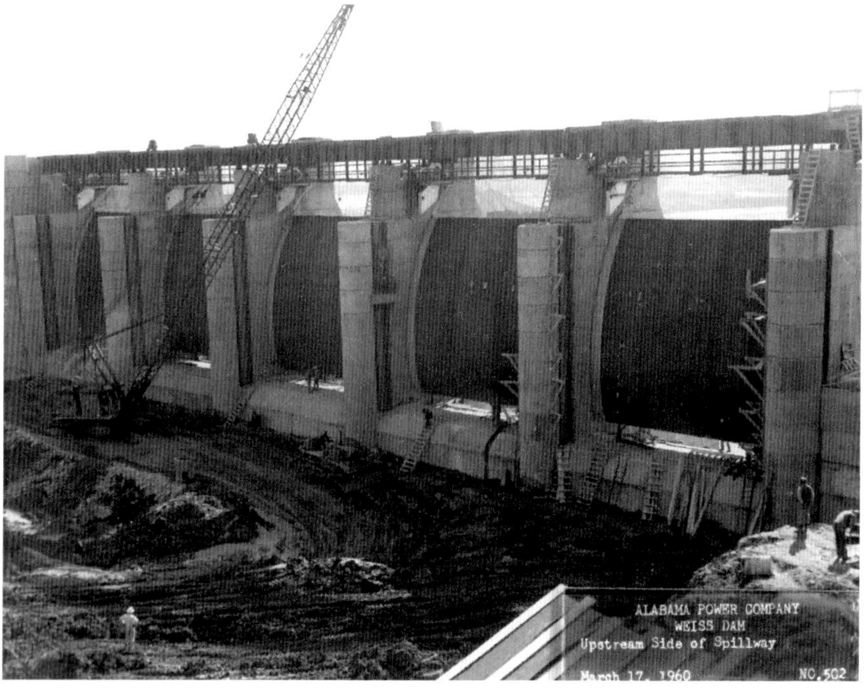

After the spillway gates were installed, construction began on the roadway that passes over the top of the dam. *Courtesy of Alabama Power Company.*

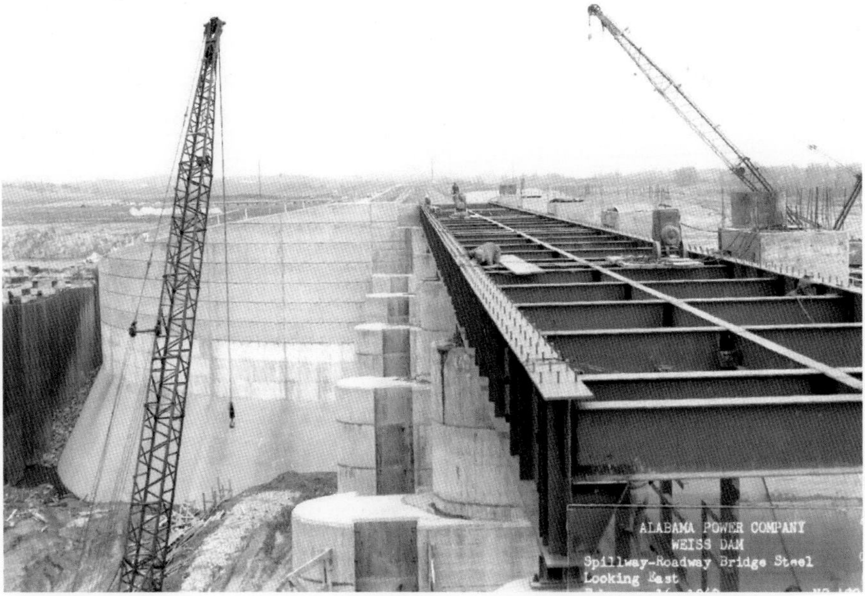

Workers place and weld steel I-beams to form the base of County Road 7 over the spillway. The road connects Leesburg to the Pollard's Bend community. *Courtesy of Alabama Power Company.*

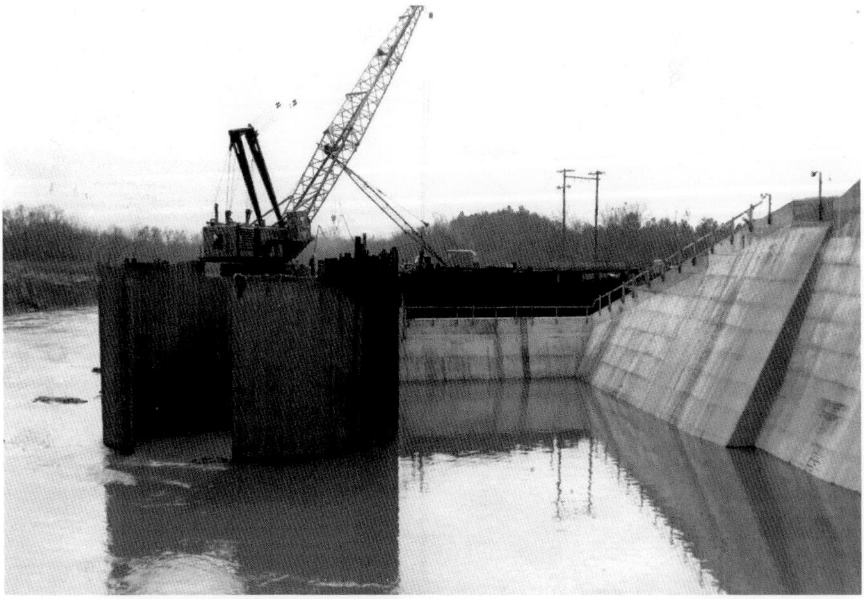

Removal of the cofferdam enclosure around the spillway began in February 1960. *Courtesy of Alabama Power Company.*

of virtual completion," read *The Em-Kayan*, "came on June 16 when first water was sent over the five-gated structure, allowing final river diversion operations." By August, with concrete work at both sites completed, photos in *The Em-Kayan* showed a row of four-cubic-yard concrete buckets being repainted in preparation for shipment to another construction site. The completed concrete portion of the powerhouse appeared in another photo. Cranes could be seen erecting the steel beams that would compose the superstructure. In December, a photo on the front page of the *Herald* showed an aerial view of the completed spillway dam that "is now being used to cross Coosa River by traffic from Leesburg to Pollard's Bend." The old Highway 411 bridge, clearly visible in the background, was still being used to cross the river into Leesburg, though concrete pilings for the new bridge could be seen rising in the still-narrowed river channel. A photo on the front page of the December 28 *Herald* showed the approaches of the new Coosa River bridge in Cedar Bluff. The caption proclaimed that it, "along with relocation of highways…will afford new streets for the town to grow with."

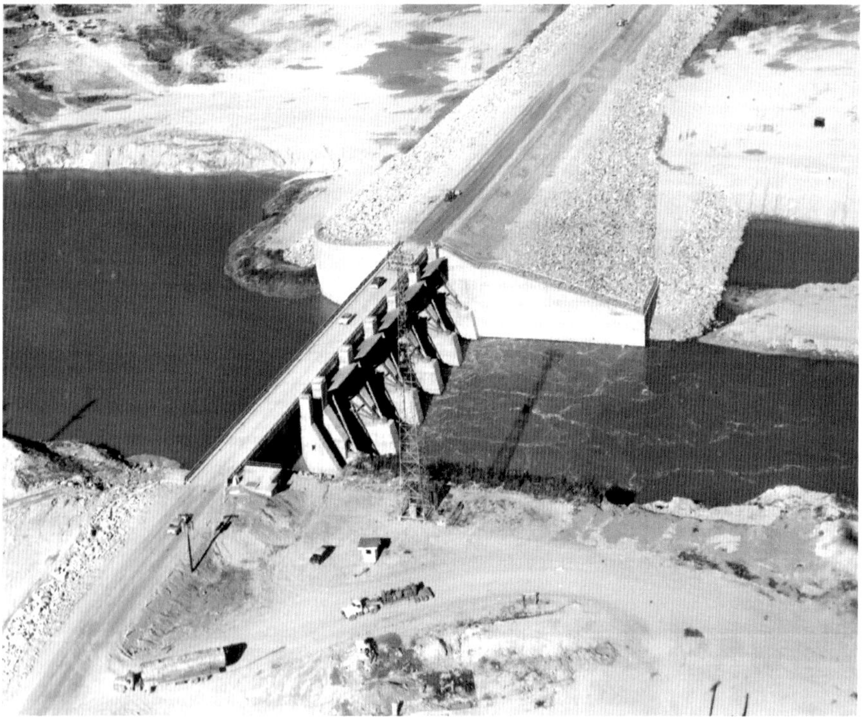

The completed spillway with traffic passing overheard on October 24, 1960. A section of the closed-off diversion channel is visible in the upper right. *Courtesy of Alabama Power Company.*

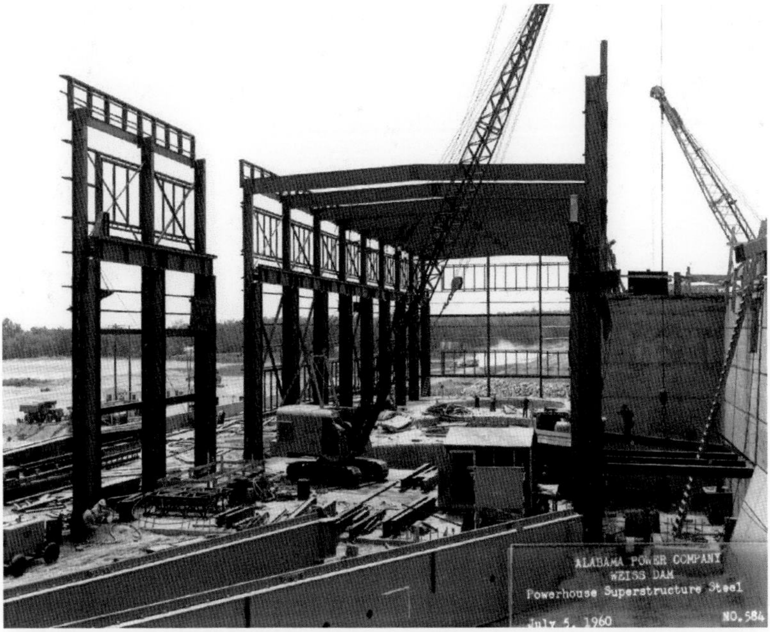

Installation of the steel superstructure of the powerhouse was underway by July 1960. *Courtesy of Alabama Power Company.*

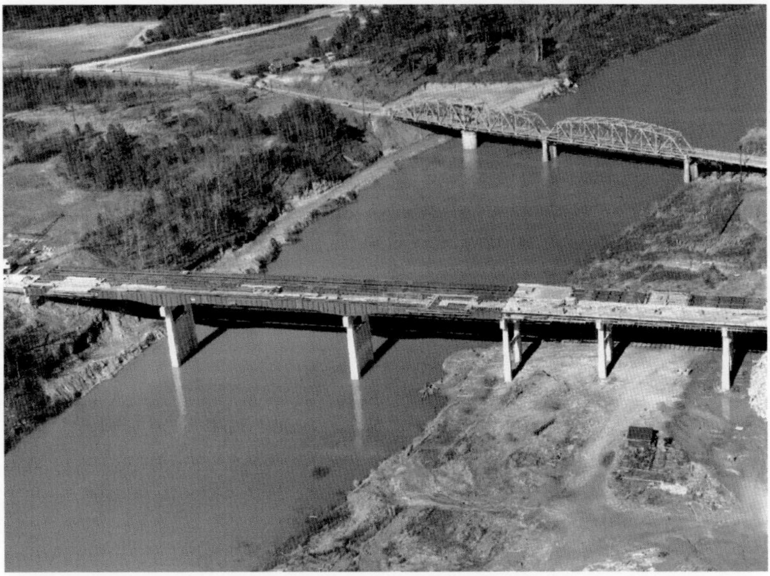

The new Highway 411 bridge was nearly complete in January 1961. Note the swivel design of the original bridge, still in place a few hundred yards upstream. It was practically identical to the John Pelham Bridge in Cedar Bluff. *Courtesy of Alabama Power Company.*

While crews at either end of the sprawling construction site busied themselves cleaning tools and implements and packing up to head to Morrison-Knudsen's next job, earthmover and bulldozer drivers in between them were hard at work putting the finishing touches on the powerhouse intake canal. Gossett remembered huge pieces of equipment crisscrossing the site "like piss ants." *The Em-Kayan* declared that the total amount of earth excavated for the canal was in excess of 2.1 million cubic yards, much of which was used to create the dikes that today protect populated areas of the county from potential flooding.

After the intake canal connecting the river to the twenty-four-hundred-acre powerhouse forebay was completed in early 1961, Alabama Power engineers began the process of final testing. A few months later, when the first turbine spun into action on June 1, the final step in the permanent alteration of both the landscape and the future of Cherokee County was complete. Water had begun to crawl into the creek bottoms and seep over dozens of abandoned roadbeds, and thousands of acres of farmland were slowly consumed by the river. Locals who had stood on opposite sides of the fight over the construction of Weiss Lake now had a decision to make: they could pull together and try to make the reservoir work for everyone in the community, or they could go their separate ways and allow a potentially priceless tourist attraction to go to waste.

THE FIRST TWENTY-FIVE YEARS

You're invited to spend a day, a week, a lifetime in Cherokee County.
—Promotional ad sponsored by the Centre Chamber of Commerce in the Gadsden Times, *May 1964*

On June 7, 1961, Alabama Power ran a three-quarter-page advertisement in the *Cherokee County Herald* announcing that the Weiss Dam powerhouse was officially online. "We consider ourselves to be a part of the community," the power company proudly declared. On July 19, the front page of the *Herald* introduced the new operation to the community with an up-close photograph of the powerhouse control room and its multiple banks of switches, dials, control arms and recording equipment. In August, state senator George Godfrey announced that bridges nearing completion over the Coosa River in Leesburg and Cedar Bluff had been named, and signs would soon be erected. Later that month, in an opinion column, *Herald* columnist Dixie Miller predicted that the population of Leesburg would quickly reach five thousand and that the town was "destined, perhaps, to become the metropolis of Cherokee County."

Whether it was because they had no other option, or because they were genuinely excited to have something to do in the summertime other than hoe weeds in a cotton field, the more forward-looking members of the community took to Weiss Lake right away. Near the end of June, around the same time traffic in Cedar Bluff was rerouted onto the newly named John L. Burnett Bridge, Mr. and Mrs. Buddy Bedwell opened the Bedwell Boat Dock Café near the end of the eastern approach. Possibly in anticipation of carloads of hungry out-of-towners, Hobart Keasler opened the Dari Chief on Highway 9 in Centre in October, where he and his wife handed out

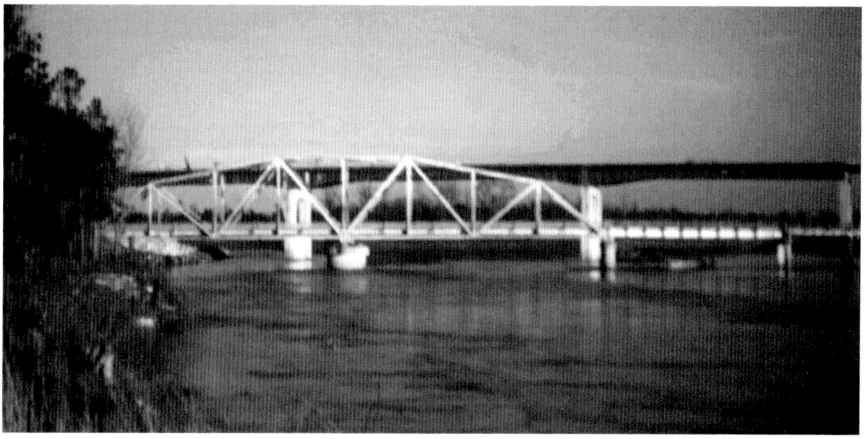

A new concrete and steel bridge (background) over the Coosa River in Cedar Bluff opened in 1961. When this photo was taken, the old bridge was still open to traffic. *Courtesy of Sue Young.*

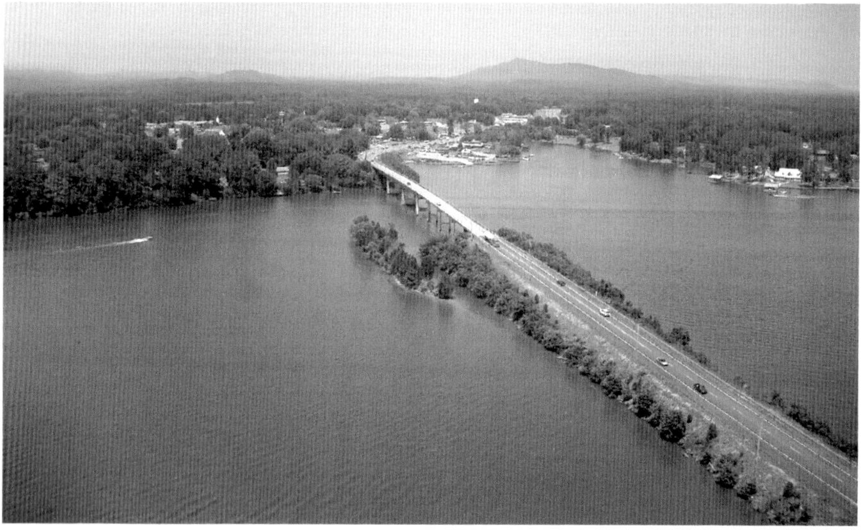

The 967-foot-long John L. Burnett Bridge, which opened to traffic in 1961, connects Cedar Bluff and Centre. Note the old roadbed, now overgrown with trees. *Courtesy of Jimmy Wallace.*

homemade cheeseburgers for nineteen cents and foot-long hotdogs for a nickel more. The following month, a couple of miles away on West Main Street in Centre, D.H. Powell and his son Phil opened the Centre Motel. Comprising prefabricated suites constructed in Michigan, the motel featured sixteen units, wall-to-wall carpeting, TV and phone service and access to an all-night mechanic. Just north of Cedar Bluff, near the mouth of Little River, Bob Baker and his wife Martha opened a marina that would quickly become one of the most popular fishing spots on Weiss Lake.

In the summer of 1961, the *Herald* announced that a pair of secondary bridges would soon be built across the Coosa River for the first time—one at Garrett's Ferry and the other at McClusky's Ferry. The bridges, to be paid for with federal, state and county funds, would provide a "direct route through the populous, highly-developed agricultural area of Pollard's Bend to East Gadsden." By the middle of December, construction had begun on the new Centre Municipal Airport, another first for the county. (There were other, more ignominious firsts associated with Cherokee County's new role as a recreation destination. When Centre resident Herman Brown's boat capsized near Leesburg on June 27, 1961, the forty-two-year-old World War II veteran became the first person to drown in Weiss Lake.)

On July 1, 1961 the county government joined with the City of Centre to stage boat races featuring professional racers from across the Southeast competing in three categories. Spectators lunched on barbecue sandwiches prepared by the Centre Quarterback Club and eyeballed Betty Scroggins, the first-ever Miss Weiss Lake, who was selected from a field of ninety-nine contestants at a beauty pageant in the National Guard armory the night before. In the July 5 edition, the *Herald* declared the boat races a "tremendous success" and noted that Collinsville native Bill Robertson brought home the first-place trophy in the professional hydroplane division.

The excitement level in Cherokee County in the first years after Weiss Lake was completed intensified throughout the 1960s. In March 1962, in order to be prepared for any lake-related emergencies, the Cherokee County Rescue Squad began sending members to Gadsden to become licensed scuba divers. Over the Labor Day weekend that year, there was a ski show on the powerhouse forebay portion of the lake. Entertainment was provided by, among others, the Warriors Ski Club. New local radio station WEIS-AM broadcast the event live. Throughout the decade, the *Herald*'s front page regularly featured photos of weighted-down stringers of brim, crappie, bass and catfish, often caught near Bay Springs Fish Camp and Trailer Park. Among the first local fishermen to see their catches documented for posterity on the *Herald*'s front page were Hal Johnson and Dr. James Burns,

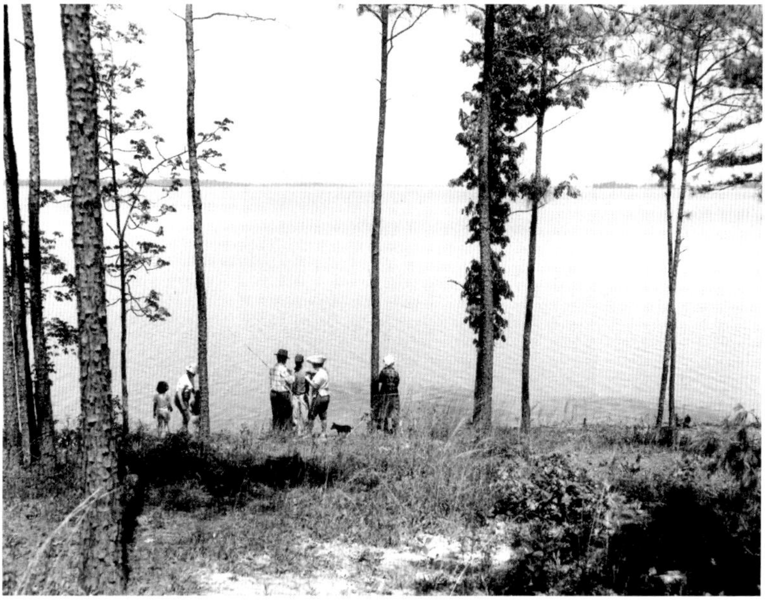

It wasn't long after Weiss Lake reached full pool in 1962 that fishermen—and fisherwomen—flocked to the banks and loaded stringers with bass and crappie. *Courtesy of the Cherokee County Public Library.*

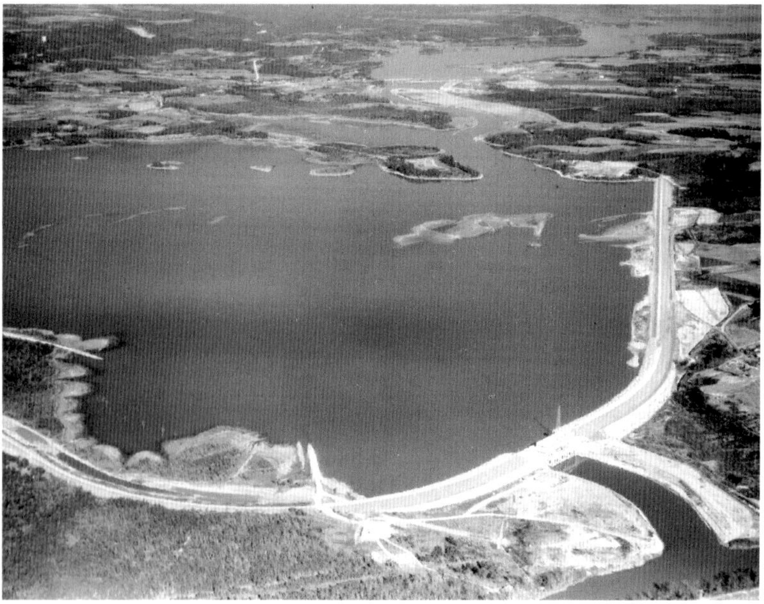

An aerial view of the twenty-four-hundred-acre forebay and intake canal, which divert the Coosa to the powerhouse before returning it to the main river channel. *Courtesy of the Cherokee County Public Library.*

who caught twenty-six pounds of fish near Bay Springs, including a five-pound bass. An editorial column later that month encouraged Cherokee County citizens to concentrate on "wooing" tourists by offering crafts and services unique to the area, such as "quilts, canned fruits, lake cruises, a tourism information center, and a family resort area." Articles in the paper frequently focused on boating safety. Advertisements offered house plans for ultramodern beach villas and rustic log cabins, both targeted at would-be weekenders and billed as "the ideal waterfront getaway." Occasionally, newspapers updated readers on the latest attempts by lawmakers to move ahead with the promised navigation locks. By that time, though, little hope remained that the Rome-to-Mobile channel was ever going to become a reality. Instead, the people of Cherokee County focused on aspects of their new surroundings that they could control.

Alabama Highway Department Director Sam Engelhart toured Cherokee County with state representative Ralph Meade and other local officials in mid-July 1961 to check on the progress of $9 million worth of secondary bridges and other road improvement projects recently begun by the state and county. Engelhart spoke of plans to widen Highway 411 between Leesburg and Centre to four lanes; another 5.6-mile stretch of two-lane road atop the new causeway between Centre and Cedar Bluff had already been completed. Meade remembered that the power company paid for only a few of the larger bridges—the Highway 411 bridge in Leesburg and the Highway 9 bridge in Cedar Bluff were the two most prominent contributions—and recalled exactly how the county acquired the funds for the other projects. Meade said he and several local officials made a trip to Montgomery in 1959 to ask for state money to build a series of bridges that would reconnect communities isolated by the new reservoir:

> *I carried the county commission, and I told them that I thought we had it made. Well, we got into the meeting and Mr. Sam Engelhart looked at me and said there was nobody that he and the governor would like to help more than the people of Cherokee County. But he said the state simply didn't have any more money to spend. After the meeting ended, I was still over there, just sort of moping around and picking up my stuff, and I had tears in my eyes. Mr. Engelhart came over to me and said, "Ralph, son, wait a minute. Does this mean that much to you?" And I told him it was going to devastate our county if we didn't get what we asked for. "We're dead," I told him. "This will kill Cherokee County." So he called me back in his office and said he'd see what he could do. And we ended up getting all nine million dollars to get those bridges. If we hadn't, the county would have been split in half.*

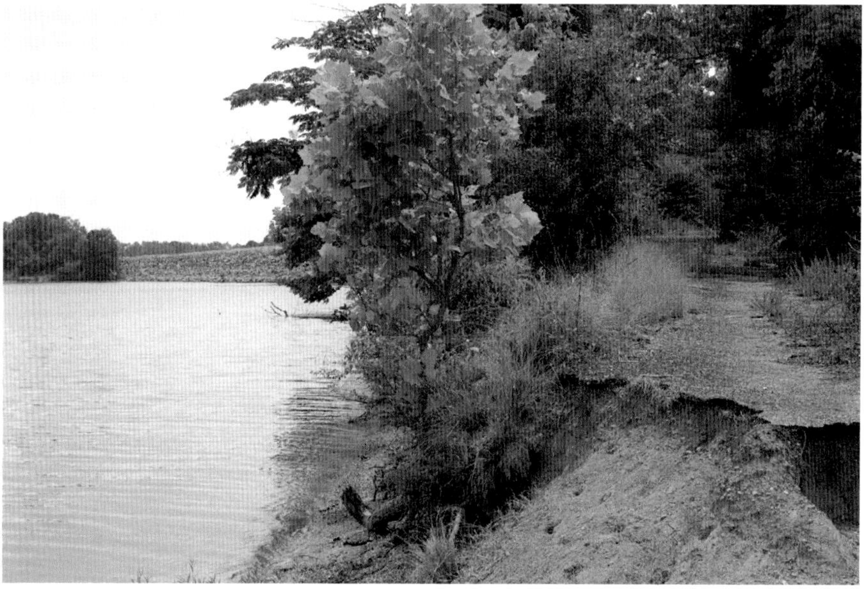

Today there is little left of the old Highway 411 roadbed near Leesburg. The east diversion dike, which extends as far as County Road 520, is visible in the background. *Photo by the author.*

Although the county's population dropped by nearly a thousand between 1960 and 1970 (from 16,303 to 15,606), partly due to the migration of sharecroppers whose farmland was lost to the lake, farming as a whole did not suffer as much as those who opposed construction of the lake in the 1950s had feared. In April 1962, the *Herald* reported that the Public Gin Company, operated by Mack Garrett, was upgrading its equipment and would be able to handle as many as three hundred bales of cotton every twenty-four hours. Garrett told the newspaper that customers often came from as far as forty miles away to have their cotton ginned at his facility. In June 1963, the *Herald* reported that Cherokee County ranked fifth among the sixty-seven counties in the state in cotton production for the previous year. According to the Alabama Department of Agriculture, local farmers averaged "466 pounds of lint on 23,600 acres." A year later, Cherokee County Agent J.J. Young told the *Gadsden Times* that cotton was still the number one crop in the county. "It accounts for 48 per cent of the gross agricultural income," Young said. "In 1963 production was approximately 500 pounds per acre on 21,277 acres." The best farmland in the county might have been covered by Weiss Lake, but it was obvious the soil still above the water line was every bit as fertile.

The *Gadsden Times* ran a special advertising section in May 1964 titled "Cherokee County Unlimited." The twenty-eight-page insert, inspired by

Times proofreader and Cherokee County resident Virginia Brock, touted the area as a recreation spot using photos of young, attractive men and women relaxing on Weiss Lake. "You're invited to spend a day, a week, a lifetime in Cherokee County," announced a full-page ad placed by the Centre Chamber of Commerce. The towns of Centre, Cedar Bluff, Leesburg and Gaylesville all sponsored eye-grabbing advertisements encouraging out-of-towners to consider Weiss Lake for weekend getaways. The special section also trumpeted the community's latest improvements, including several new boat launches, marinas and restaurants. Among them was Bob's Fish Camp, which featured three acres of gravel parking space; the Ellis Lighthouse Restaurant in Cedar Bluff, where patrons could "dine privately in the Bamboo Room"; and the Dari Queen in east Centre, where it was always "Top Banana Time." The *Herald* reported that during the time Paul and Jack Ellis owned the Lighthouse, they prepared meals for visitors "from every state in the Union including Alaska and from a number of foreign countries including Holland, Italy, England, Germany, Japan, and Puerto Rico." If customer lists at local restaurants like the Lighthouse were any indication, there was plenty of growth and prosperity on the horizon for the Weiss Lake area.

By 1968, a five-lane stretch of Highway 9 from the Cherokee County Courthouse toward Cedar Bluff was complete, and clearing had begun for construction of the promised four-lane section of Highway 411 between Centre and Leesburg. If tourists wanted to visit Weiss Lake to splash in the water or reel in a mess of fish, then local officials, working through state and federal agencies, were determined to do their part to ensure easy automobile access. In early June of '68, Illinois natives Marvin and Katie Oliver purchased the already-successful Little River Marina and began "steadily making improvements to increase the popularity of Weiss Lake as a resort area." Over the Labor Day weekend, the Centre Chamber of Commerce sponsored an all-day boat ride to Mayo's Bar near Rome, Georgia, and back as a way to encourage visitors and residents alike to think of Weiss Lake whenever they sought recreational opportunities or a tranquil place to relax.

On February 2, 1972, Cherokee County Extension Chairman Howard Hall announced that county farmers had grossed $16.7 million from the sale of agricultural products the previous year, an increase of $2 million over 1970. "Cotton growers had their greatest year yet," the *Herald* reported. "Gross returns soared to $7.69 million, as compared to $5.67 million in 1970." The next month, the *Herald* reported that the U.S. Department of Commerce had counted 1,062 farms in Cherokee County with an average size of 160.2 acres and an average value of over $31,000. But while the community's excitement grew as farming output exceeded pre-lake levels, the enthusiasm over Alabama Power's new reservoir began to diminish. With the exception of a photograph of Centre youths Shad Ellis and Phil Jordan holding aloft a stringer of crappie on March 22, there was little lake-related news in the newspaper in '72. After a decade of efforts to "woo" tourists to Cherokee County, a community that had been dominated by farming for over a hundred years seemed increasingly determined to return to its roots.

By 1974, front-page coverage of Weiss had almost completely disappeared. There was a list of winners of a bass rodeo in the May 1 edition of the *Herald*, notice of an upcoming crappie tournament at Cherokee Camper Site on May 5 and a picture of Pat Allen's stringer of large catfish on October 30. Possibly, the lack of Weiss-related coverage in the local paper had less to do with the editorial staff's priorities than with a community-wide lack of excitement about the lake. Instead of a local club or organization, it was the Rossville Jaycees that sponsored a successful bass rodeo at Cherokee Camper Site in June. Local attorney Dean Buttram Jr. was active in the county in the 1970s and recalled the time when the novelty of the lake began to fade:

> *After the lake was completed there was a decade or so of great enthusiasm that overwhelmed the people. Word about the county got out. But after that the excitement kind of wore off. I think it was just a kind of natural lull that occurred, like a fad. Some of that was associated with the bad press about the condition of the river and the fish. But there was also a bit of falling off in our sales of the county and the lake.*

By the mid-1970s, photos of stringers of fish seldom made the news. Instead, occasional mentions of crappie and bass hauls were relegated to the back pages, often stuffed into the sports section or crammed alongside the classifieds. In 1975, the March 5 edition did include a full-page report prepared by Colonel Claude Smith that discussed the lake's tourism potential, but it wasn't very complimentary. Among Smith's conclusions were that "facilities in Cherokee County for tourists are quite limited and are aimed principally at daytime fishermen." He added that the county would be well advised to take advantage of its prime location and pointed out that there were "some three million persons in surrounding areas and a fine interstate highway within a few miles."

In between atrocious photographs of local businessmen in leisure suits, high school graduates in gaudy, oversized bowties and politicians sheathed in runaway sideburns, news stories in the summer of 1976 revolved around the nation's bicentennial celebration, Centre's newly paved tennis courts and groundbreaking for the new Farmers & Merchants Bank building on West Main Street. The only front-page mention the lake warranted all year announced the creation of the Weiss Lake Fishing Club, which organized in August during a meeting at Bay Springs. Noah Gladden was the club's first president; among the other charter members were Bert Latham, Terrell Ransum and Joe Rattray.

Perhaps spurred on by a well-attended meeting of the Cherokee County Tourism Association in January, news reports about the lake enjoyed a brief resurgence in 1977. The group's officers, including president Tommy Oliver and vice president Tom Harton, discussed their growing concerns over the pollution making its way into the lake from Georgia. They also announced plans to print 100,000 four-color, tri-fold brochures featuring the first-ever map of Weiss Lake and a listing of prominent tourist spots in the county. As the *Herald* reported, the association's plans called for the advertisements to be distributed to travel agents and motor clubs across the country, and at highway rest stops, motels and other public places in Alabama.

Oliver and his wife, Nell, owners of Little River Marina at the time, said a series of negative news reports in the mid-1970s concerning the discovery of polychlorinated biphenyls in the Coosa River left parking lots at marinas like theirs virtually empty. "After the PCB scare, it was a while before the out-of-state fishermen started coming back," he said. Oliver said news of PCB contamination in Weiss "got all over the Southeast," and it took the Tourist Association a lot of time, effort and expense to generate favorable publicity and fight for the economic future of the county. "We did it on our own. It was hard to counter all of those negative headlines," he said. Nell Oliver remembered how they and a few others went about trying to change the lake's image:

> *The Cherokee County Tourist Association was begun in 1975 because of the PCBs. Everything was just dying. J. W. Hampton called us about getting it started, and Tom Harton and Bob Baker helped a lot. Ken Mackey, too. There were many others involved, from all over the county. We went to a convention and met a man who wrote for Bassmasters magazine, and the article he wrote after he came up here and fished a couple of times generated calls to the marina for years. That was one of the best things that came from the Tourist Association.*

Nell Oliver said the group worked hard for a handful of years to promote Weiss Lake and then "died out" after the PCB story dropped off the front pages and boat traffic on the lake returned to normal. Still, by the time 1980 rolled around, it often seemed that news about Weiss Lake was either bad or nonexistent. There were two drowning victims in June—one near Sand Valley and another involving a man from Georgia. A few weeks later, a Cherokee County High School student drowned near Spring Creek. In November, forty-four-year-old Brice Morgan escaped serious injury after he ran his car into the lake near Yellow Creek. The news about the Tourist Association's tireless efforts to revive the tourist trade and several consecutive good crappie seasons did not make front-page news. Instead, in July 1980, *Herald* readers were encouraged to recreate out of town at a newly opened wave pool several hours away in Decatur.

As the 1980s began, Weiss Lake still had not become the catalyst for unparalleled economic growth that Alabama Power executives and Washington politicians predicted at the Leesburg groundbreaking in April 1958. Factories never flocked to the area to take advantage of an easily accessible water supply or cheap electricity, which wasn't available in TVA-supplied Cherokee County, anyway. As is often the case with elected officials, repeated promises of funding—in this case, for navigation locks on the Coosa—went unfulfilled. Cherokee County was the recently named "Crappie Capital of the World" and little else. It seemed there were only a few dedicated locals who cared about even that lone distinction, at least until 1982.

THE LAST TWENTY-FIVE YEARS

I think the water quality has gotten better over the years, although we still have a long way to go.
—Weiss Lake Improvement Association President Carolyn Landrem, July 2008

J.R. Tucker

When Jerry "J.R." Tucker and his wife, Geraldine, bought the Little River Marina in early 1982 and renamed it J.R.'s Marina, there was already a renewed interest in fishing in Weiss Lake thanks to several consecutive good crappie fishing seasons and the efforts of the Cherokee County Tourist Association. Tucker, a construction company owner and avid fisherman with a flair for public relations, immediately set about promoting the lake in new and creative ways. Carolyn Landrem, current president of the Weiss Lake Improvement Association (WLIA), a nonprofit organization dedicated to preserving and enhancing Weiss Lake, said Tucker was truly one of a kind:

> *I think J.R. had a unique marketing skill, and that was his ability to go out and catch fish. When the PCB ban ended, I think J.R. and others in the community really did some things that helped market the lake in the mid-1980s. He had an ability to give people a good experience on the lake, and when those fishermen got home they would tell a friend, who would tell another friend. And word-of-mouth is the best kind of advertising there is.*

J.R. and Geraldine both passed away recently, she in November 2006 and he a few months later. Today, sons Curt and Jason run the marina and

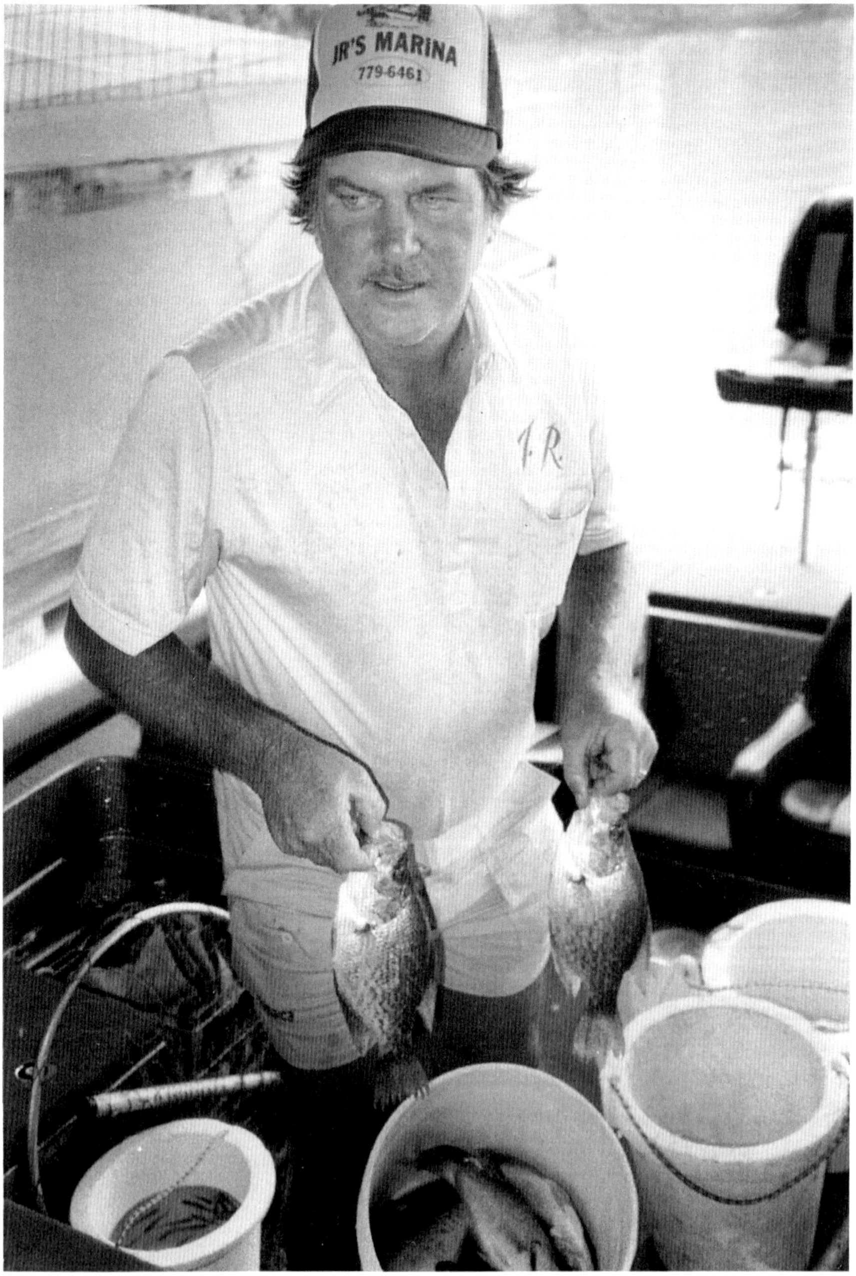

Jerry "J.R." Tucker was among a growing handful of dedicated fishermen and business owners who reinvigorated the tourist trade in Cherokee County in the early 1980s. *Courtesy of Curt and Jason Tucker.*

adjoining boat shop with a passion passed down from their parents. "Daddy may have said he closed down a half-day for Christmas, but he didn't. He was here," Curt Tucker said. "They worked seven days a week." At the funeral, Curt said he realized how deeply instilled his father's love for Weiss Lake really was:

> *I talked to people he went to school with, graduated with, and they told me one of his goals was always to own a marina. That was what he wanted to do, even when he was a kid. And he really just loved the public relations side of it, the talking to people. Fishing was the bonus, for him. Daddy knew how to make money and Momma knew the business side of it. It took both of them. They worked as a team, and they loved this lake.*

Over time, the excitement generated by people like J.R. and Geraldine Tucker spread to others in the community. In the mid-1980s, Harry Stressel created a fishing organization he called Crappiethon and began staging fishing tournaments to catch and tag crappie. Thanks to newly mandated creel and size limits the Tuckers and others had been insisting upon for years, there were more and more crappie to be caught practically every year during the 1980s. After the crappie were tagged and released, they could be caught again at tournaments that brought in fishermen by the hundreds to compete for prizes ranging from a few dollars to a new fishing boat. J.R.'s son, Jason, is one of over a dozen fishing guides who today operate from marinas and boat launches across Cherokee County. Fishermen drive from halfway across the country to float across the predawn surface of Weiss Lake and reel in largemouth and smallmouth bass, or a live well filled with a mess of those coveted crappie.

Weiss Lake Improvement Association

One of the many ways the Tuckers, and eventually hundreds of others, showed their commitment to the long-term success of the county's tourist-driven economy was through involvement in the nonprofit Weiss Lake Improvement Association (WLIA), founded in 1997. The WLIA started out as a committee formed by the Cherokee County Chamber of Commerce. Originally tasked to devise a way to better promote the lake, the group became a permanent fixture after its report was completed and committee members realized they needed an organized push if they ever hoped to see the recommendations implemented. "Since that time, the group's goal has always been to protect the quality of the water and the fisheries and enhance the lake, so that it will always be a good economic stimulus for the county," said Carolyn Landrem.

Over the past decade, WLIA has sponsored water-quality monitoring classes in conjunction with Alabama Water Watch and worked with the Rome, Georgia–based Coosa River Basin Initiative to address concerns over water levels and pollution from upstream sources. Landrem said the Tuckers and other fishermen also persuaded the group to partner with the Alabama Department of Conservation to restock dwindling fish populations earlier this decade:

> *For three years, WLIA paid to stock fish in the lake. The Department of Conservation said it would never work, that the survival rate would be so low that it wouldn't be economically viable. But when they started conducting studies, they found out the restocking was working. The survival rate was much higher than they anticipated. And their commitment to us is that they will continue to stock fish in the lake as long as we have poor spawn years. We've had poor spawns for the past three years and I anticipate another this year, due to the drought. We have good spawns in the years when we have flood situations.*

Landrem said WLIA also works with Alabama Power and county and municipal governments to conduct an annual week-long cleanup of the lake as part of the statewide Renew Our Rivers campaign. "That's the big annual cleanup and it's a big part of what we do," Landrem said. "We have more students and people involved in our cleanup than any other lake in the state has because we involve the schoolchildren in the process." WLIA also worked with Alabama Power and the U.S. Army Corps of Engineers (ACOE) in 2004–05 to write a new licensing agreement for Weiss Lake, as Alabama Power's original fifty-year license to operate the dam was set to expire in 2007. "One of changes in the agreement was that instead of dropping the water level six feet in the winter, Alabama Power would only drop it three feet, and they'd also get the lake to full pool a month sooner in the spring and keep it at full pool a month longer in the fall." But Landrem said when the new language in the agreement regarding winter lake levels reached the ACOE in 2005, the agency unexpectedly declined to approve the license. Suddenly, the ACOE claimed, an obscure, fifty-five-year-old document detailing flood control procedures for the Coosa River needed to be rewritten:

> *I never understood how the ACOE was involved in the whole process and then, at the last minute, claimed they had to re-write their entire manual. It's all political, I think. All of that happened right after Alabama Power joined in a lawsuit against the ACOE and the state of Georgia. So we're still operating under the old license and will be for some time, I imagine.*

In August 2008, the Corps of Engineers finally announced plans to hold a series of meetings to allow the public to voice concerns about delays in rewriting the water control manual. Alabama Power officials said that, barring further setbacks, they expect the company's new license to operate Weiss Dam for another fifty years to be approved by the Federal Energy Regulatory Commission by 2010.

Water Quality

Perhaps it is just as well that the long-promised navigation locks—the highlight of stump speeches by Representative Albert Rains and other eager politicians for decades—were never added to Alabama Power's hydroelectric dams along the upper Coosa. If the river had been made navigable and large-scale industrial operations constructed manufacturing plants along its banks, there is a chance that no one would be allowed anywhere near Weiss Lake today for fear of being poisoned.

According to a study compiled by Auburn University professor David R. Bayne in 1995, water quality became an issue in the Coosa River a decade before construction of Weiss Lake began. In 1948, the newly created Alabama Water Improvement Commission (AWIC) found the river near Cedar Bluff to be "moderately polluted" with organic waste. In 1955, nine months after Rome Kraft Company went into operation near Rome, Georgia, a significant decline in dissolved oxygen (DO) was detected in the Coosa that extended "over fifty miles into Alabama." Two years later, another study found that DO levels extended even farther downstream than previously detected. Within a few months after Weiss Dam began operation in 1961, the *Cherokee County Herald* reported the lake's first significant fish kill, likely caused by pollution dumped into the Coosa and Chattooga Rivers on the Georgia side of the state line. The following year, during a special session of the Alabama legislature, both the House and Senate asked Georgia officials to take action to prevent further contamination.

After the State of Georgia failed to address the problem, the U.S. Public Health Service became involved and quickly discovered that the Chattooga

River was "grossly polluted by municipal sewage and industrial wastes" at levels that made "water contact recreation unadvisable." The federal study ultimately concluded that wastes entering the two rivers before they emptied into Weiss Lake "endanger the health and welfare of persons in Alabama." In 1969, further testing of the Coosa River downstream from Rome showed continued levels of "serious pollution" that deteriorated further as the river flowed past Inland-Rome and a Georgia Power Company steam plant a few miles farther downstream. A study conducted by the Environmental Protection Agency in 1973 found Weiss Lake to be the most contaminated of eleven Alabama lakes surveyed. Three years later, the Georgia Department of Natural Resources collected fish from the Coosa near Mayo's Bar and discovered an alarming level of polychlorinated biphenyls (PCBs) had seeped into the river from a General Electric transformer plant in Rome. The discovery resulted in a fish consumption advisory involving every species of fish in Weiss Lake. A follow-up study conducted by the Alabama Department of Environmental Management in 1988 found continued unsafe PCB levels in channel catfish, resulting in a second limited health advisory.

Another problem Weiss Lake has faced for decades, primarily because of its relatively shallow depth (10.2 feet at full pool on average) and significant amount of shoreline, is the level of nutrient enrichment in the water. According to a report prepared by the Cherokee County Chamber of Commerce for the county commission in 1996, Weiss Lake "receives non-point source nutrients from feedlots and animal management areas and siltation from cropland erosion," rendering the lake excessively eutrophic. A reservoir that exhibits eutrophic qualities, the report explained, is characterized as being "rich in nutrients which cause excessive growth of aquatic plants, especially algae; the resulting bacteria consumes nearly all the oxygen, especially during warm weather, choking fish, etc."

Considering that there have been so many instances of significant levels of man-made pollution entering Weiss Lake over the years, the lack of federal funds to build navigation locks may have been a blessing in disguise for Cherokee County. Had a few additional manufacturing plants been lured to the area in the late 1950s and early 1960s by the promise of cheap waterborne transportation to the Gulf of Mexico, the resulting industrial waste, combined with the present flow of contaminates, might have been more than the Coosa River could handle.

Carolyn Landrem acknowledged that there have been significant water quality issues in the past but said her organization is working to make sure potential problems, some old and some new, no longer go overlooked, even if correcting them sometimes seems nearly impossible:

> *The water quality is actually better today, and I think people who are out on the lake on a regular basis can tell the quality is better than it used to be. We had the issue with PCBs several years ago, and with industries in Georgia putting things in the water that end up down here, and that's not good. But I think the water quality has gotten better over the years, although we still have a long way to go. Actually, sedimentation is the biggest issue we face right now.*

Landrem explained that sediment levels rise when dirt from construction sites and other poorly protected shoreline projects wash into the lake and settle on the bottom. "There are areas in this lake that you could have easily navigated five years ago but you cannot navigate today when it comes down to winter pool because of the sedimentation." Past PCB contaminations complicate the problem, she said: "Those PCBs are still in the lake, they're just covered up. So, there is no dredging allowed because that would stir up the PCBs. It's a Catch-22."

Economic Impact

The most recent study, conducted by the A.L. Burress Institute of Public Service at Kennesaw State University in 1995, found that Weiss Lake generated an annual economic impact of over $200 million in Cherokee County. The study likened the lake's financial effects to "a manufacturing plant employing at least 1,200 employees" that also "enhances the value of land and homes in the community and attracts growth and development." The report also warned against complacency that could endanger the economic benefits of the lake and made several recommendations:

> *Like any resource or investment, the lake's capacity to generate economic development has to be protected and enhanced to ensure that it will continue to serve as an engine for future growth of the community.*

In response to the Kennesaw State study, a pair of reports was prepared over the next two years. Both offered specific strategies for improving the water quality in Weiss Lake and preserving its viability as a long-term economic benefit. A report by the East Alabama Planning Commission included suggestions for increasing awareness of potential pollution sources, passage of countywide building codes and the improved enforcement of sewage regulations by the local health department. Several committee members who had been involved in compiling the chamber of commerce report organized the WLIA to fight for their policy suggestions, as well. Landrem has been working with other members for four years to preserve and promote Weiss Lake and still possessed a copy of her group's report. It suggested many of the same policies proposed by the planning commission. Unfortunately, Landrem said, the protection of the county's most valuable resource has consistently remained a low priority for local governments:

> *A lot of the things that were recommended years ago, we're still trying to get done today. There's still a lack of willingness by the county and city governments to move forward with some of those things. Weiss Lake Improvement Association has no power to enact the recommendations. It's up to local government to change all that, and so far they haven't moved forward with any plans to get it done.*

WLIA's report suggested, among other improvements, the creation of a Weiss Lake Advisory Committee to organize regulatory agencies, scientists and politicians at the federal, state and local level. Also, the report recommended a public education campaign be instituted to warn about the dangers and illegalities of dumping sewage into the lake and implementing improved permitting requirements for campers and mobile homes. Over ten years after the two management and protection plans for Weiss Lake were first published, the county government—which has jurisdiction over 90 percent of the lake's 447 miles of shoreline—is still working to create plans for supervising and inspecting building projects along the waterfront.

Local real estate agent Shad Ellis said he thinks the time has come for local government to get more involved in the management of Weiss Lake, which he believes is the county's most valuable resource:

> *The first thing we need is some kind of management of countywide restrictions, which we do not have right now. I'm talking about subdivision restrictions, sewage restrictions, building codes. I think the county needs to set up some type of system to regulate those things. Compared to the cost of a home, a $500 permit would be insignificant. And I think having those restrictions in place, along with a system for enforcing them, would help coordinate the growth of this county. I see that being the biggest problem, because right now people can do anything they want.*

Thankfully, the lack of an organized effort to safeguard the long-term water quality in Weiss Lake has so far not hindered recreational development

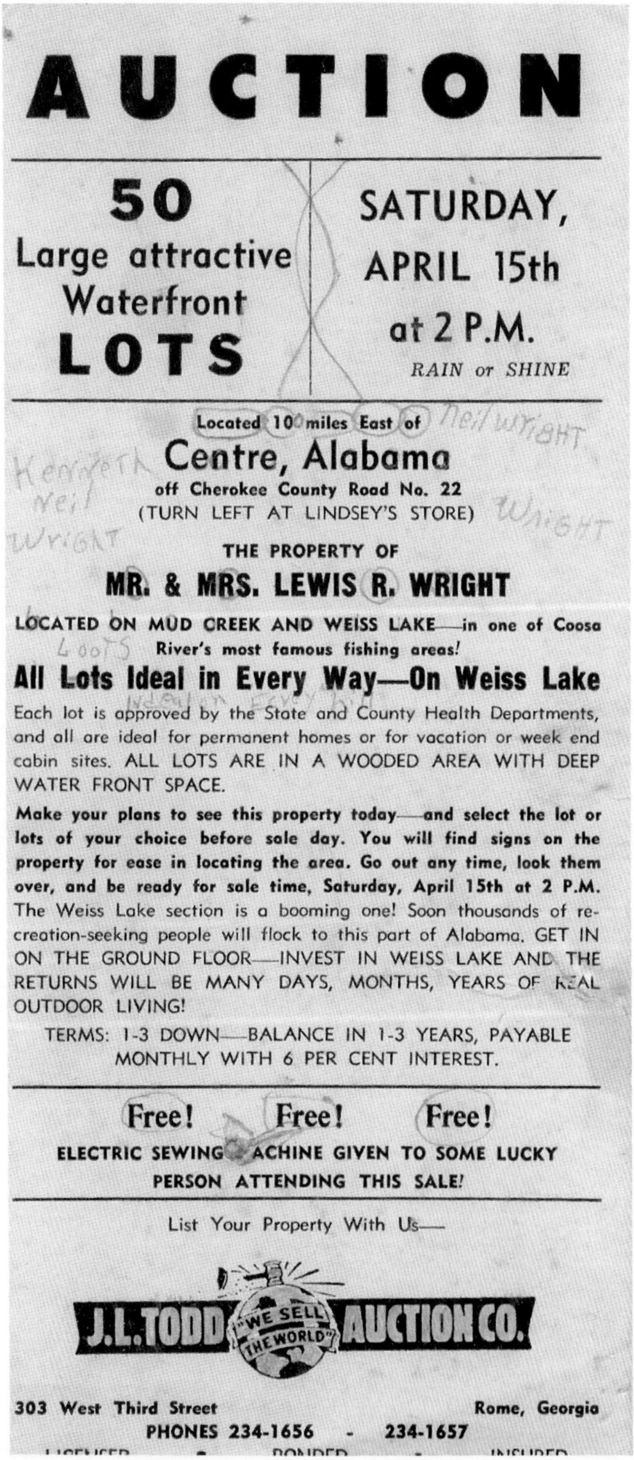

AUCTION

50 Large attractive Waterfront LOTS

SATURDAY, APRIL 15th at 2 P.M.
RAIN or SHINE

Located 10 miles East of
Centre, Alabama
off Cherokee County Road No. 22
(TURN LEFT AT LINDSEY'S STORE)

THE PROPERTY OF
MR. & MRS. LEWIS R. WRIGHT

LOCATED ON MUD CREEK AND WEISS LAKE—in one of Coosa River's most famous fishing areas!

All Lots Ideal in Every Way—On Weiss Lake

Each lot is approved by the State and County Health Departments, and all are ideal for permanent homes or for vacation or week end cabin sites. ALL LOTS ARE IN A WOODED AREA WITH DEEP WATER FRONT SPACE.

Make your plans to see this property today—and select the lot or lots of your choice before sale day. You will find signs on the property for ease in locating the area. Go out any time, look them over, and be ready for sale time, Saturday, April 15th at 2 P.M. The Weiss Lake section is a booming one! Soon thousands of recreation-seeking people will flock to this part of Alabama. GET IN ON THE GROUND FLOOR—INVEST IN WEISS LAKE AND THE RETURNS WILL BE MANY DAYS, MONTHS, YEARS OF REAL OUTDOOR LIVING!

TERMS: 1-3 DOWN—BALANCE IN 1-3 YEARS, PAYABLE MONTHLY WITH 6 PER CENT INTEREST.

Free! Free! Free!
ELECTRIC SEWING MACHINE GIVEN TO SOME LUCKY PERSON ATTENDING THIS SALE!

List Your Property With Us—

J.L. TODD "WE SELL THE WORLD" AUCTION CO.

303 West Third Street — Rome, Georgia
PHONES 234-1656 - 234-1657

At an auction in Mud Creek in the early 1960s, my grandparents sold fifty waterfront lots for an average of $750 each. My uncle Neil got bored during the auction and found a pencil. *Courtesy of Sarah Gossett Wright.*

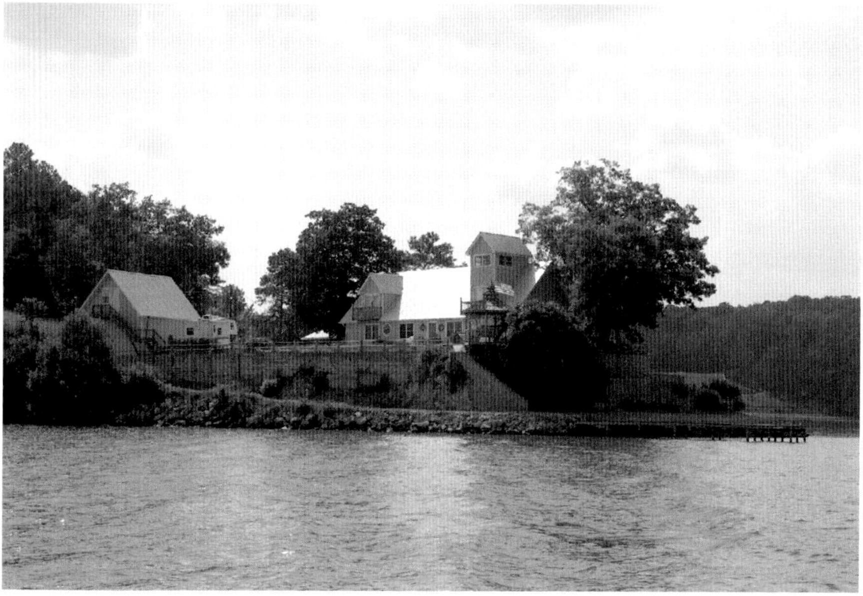

Over the past twenty years, people across the Southeast have discovered Weiss Lake. As a result, the number of expensive, custom-designed waterfront homes—and the county's tax base—increases every year. *Photo by the author.*

in Cherokee County. Since the lake was built in 1961, waterfront property values have climbed almost continually. Acre-sized lots that sold for a few hundred dollars in the early 1960s sell for over two hundred times that amount today. "I don't have any records or documentation, but people have told me about buying waterfront building lots for $700 back when the lake was first built," said Tony O'Neal, a third-generation real estate agent. "I had a guy come in once who told me my grandfather tried to talk him into buying five lots for one thousands dollars apiece. Today, those same lots are worth $200,000 each."

O'Neal said he is thankful to see investors come to Cherokee County and construct million-dollar, waterfront developments that both enhance the community and promote the area as a tourist attraction to the rest of the country:

> *The development known as the Bluffs has really helped in that respect, because they have not only promoted their property but also Weiss Lake and Cherokee County. I think that has been an asset. I think a lot of local people have been wrong to doubt the future success of places like Chesnut Bay and the condominiums in Cedar Bluff that out-of-town interests have*

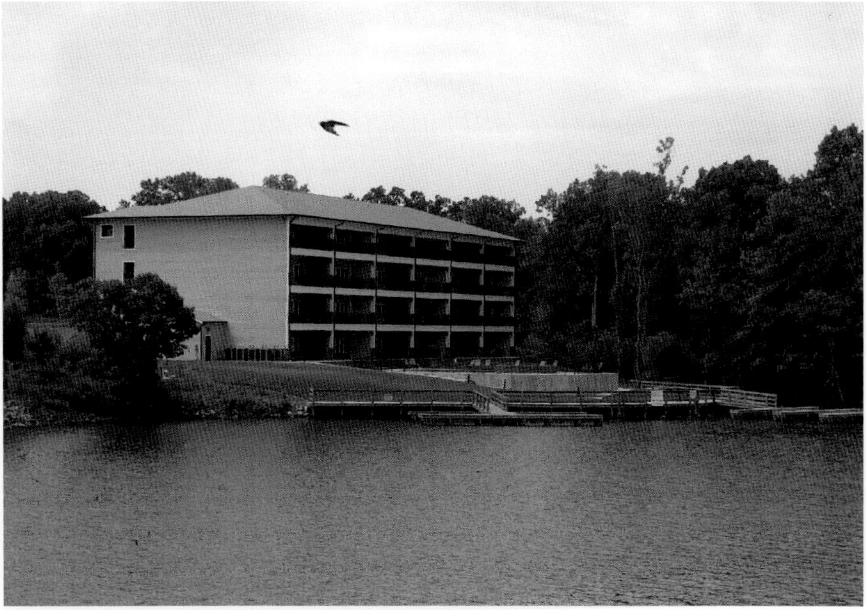

The Overlook at Weiss Lake, a twenty-four-unit condominium built by a pair of real estate developers from Georgia, opened in Cedar Bluff in 2007. *Photo by the author.*

> *built recently. When people around here think of condos they think of the Gulf of Mexico, but every day there are more and more reasons to think about Weiss Lake instead of the Gulf.*

Ellis said he, too, is happy to see the growth Weiss Lake has allowed the county to experience over the past few years. "If it wasn't for Weiss Lake, Cherokee County would be a lot like other rural counties in Alabama—lots of pine trees and cows, and literally no tax base. Lakefront lots are priced at over $200,000, and when you consider the property taxes received by the revenue office those values are immeasurable," he said. Like O'Neal, Ellis said the lake provides the local economy with a unique opportunity to capitalize on its tourism potential. He said he expects the appeal of Weiss Lake to increase in the coming years as gasoline prices force vacationers from cities such as Chattanooga, Tennessee, and Huntsville, Alabama, to begin to consider alternatives to day-long drives to the Gulf Coast:

> *I perceive that, as living expenses rise higher and higher, Weiss Lake will become more and more attractive to people who don't mind traveling*

a couple of hours as opposed to driving eight or ten hours to get to the beach. I'm talking about lake lots, recreation lots, etc. We're still the best land value of any lakefront property for 90 miles in any direction. We're fortunate to be at what I call the crossroads. If you look at a map, and draw a line from Huntsville to Atlanta, and another from Birmingham to Chattanooga, "X" marks the spot and we're the "X."

Water Wars

Another pivotal issue that could threaten the future viability of Weiss Lake is a thirty-year-old dispute between Alabama and Georgia that residents of both states know simply as the "water wars." The dispute over the Alabama-Coosa-Tallapoosa (ACT) river basin began in the 1980s, when the State of Georgia announced plans to construct additional reservoirs along several rivers, including the Oostanala and Etowah, which meet in Rome, Georgia, to form the Coosa. Specifically, Georgia officials devised a plan to supply drinking water to Atlanta by draining hundreds of millions of gallons of water per day from a lake in northwest Georgia supplied by the Etowah River. Scientists and engineers predicted that such a dramatic strain upstream would leave only a trickle flowing through the Coosa and into Weiss Lake. The resulting drop in the lake level—presently listed as 564 feet above sea level at full pool—could potentially become permanent, drastically altering the landscape of Cherokee County unless concerned parties fight back.

After years of obscurity and skimpy public information, an article in the *Rome News-Tribune* in November 1999 declared that the topic, often reported in language "seemingly designed to put a bureaucrat to sleep," was receiving renewed attention from both states. Officials in Alabama feared anew that the "fast-growing, water-guzzling metropolis" of Atlanta had devised further plans to "suck the rivers dry." In a follow-up article a few days later, reporter Jason Landers wrote that a newly suggested "massive transfer from the Coosa River basin could decimate Weiss Lake's $201 million tourist-driven economy." Georgia, Landers reported, "has proposed to cut the amount of water flowing into Weiss by 488 million gallons a day by the year 2050." Worse, the inter-basin transfer meant the water would never be returned to the Coosa River after being used and treated in Atlanta. Instead, city officials planned to dump the water into another river system, the Chattahoochee. "It could spell disaster for the lake and the regional economy," Landers added, quoting Dr. Harry McGinnis, the director of the A.L. Burruss Institute of

Public Service at Kennesaw State University. "That's a big tourism draw. There is a lot of money pumped into that economy and many, many people would lose jobs."

In a November 1999 article, *The Post*, a weekly paper in Cherokee County, reported that if Georgia officials got their way the average annual flow rate of 6,800 cubic feet per second in the Coosa River below Rome could fall below just over 1,000 cubic feet per second. "Georgia's water plan calls for a 'minimum flow' of no less than 1,200 cubic feet per second...Alabama officials suspect the minimum flow would quickly become the maximum flow." *The Post* reported that the minimum flow of the Coosa "was less than Georgia's proposed flow only 114 days during a twenty-year period from 1979 to 1998. And during the worst recorded drought of the second half of this century, in August 1986, the average flow was 1,333 cubic feet per second—higher than Georgia's current proposed minimum."

Among the problems a reduced flow into Weiss Lake might cause would be a significantly extended flow rate. Local businessman Jerry Culberson, a member of the WLIA board of directors in 1999, explained in the article that water flowed completely through Weiss Lake in around eighteen days. He said if Georgia received the amount of water it wanted, flow time through the reservoir could take as long as forty-five days. The article in *The Post* continued:

> *Combined with lower levels in the river, that could lead to stagnant pools of water in low-lying areas of the reservoir where algae would thrive. These algae growths would, in turn, consume massive amounts of oxygen in the water, leaving too little to keep bass, crappie and other fish species alive.*

Attempts at negotiations to resolve the water dispute have been held several times over the years. The sessions all began with public promises of renewed cooperation between the state-appointed negotiators. Each time, they ended in an impasse, with no solutions reached or compromises seriously considered. Alabama Power, which long resisted pleas from environmental groups to become involved in the dispute, recently began to lobby publicly for protection of the Coosa River system. Today, advocates for both sides fear the case may eventually end up before the United States Supreme Court, but to date that fear—of an impartial decision rendered by an objective third party—has done nothing to hasten attempts to reach a solution that would ensure the long-term economic vitality of the Coosa River Basin while satisfying Atlanta's undying thirst. Hopefully, the people

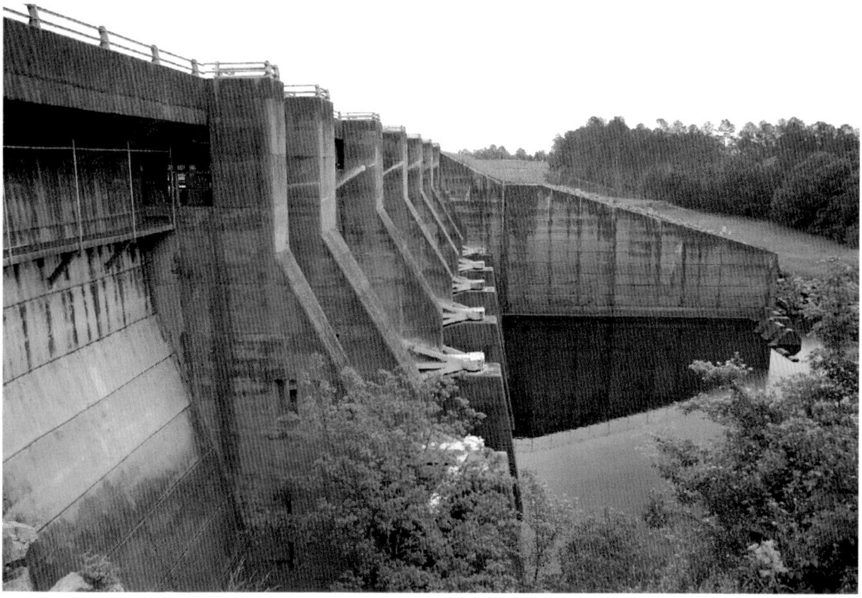

The Weiss Dam spillway today. *Photo by the author.*

who currently call Cherokee County home, many of them the offspring of farmers who had their lives forever altered by the creation of Weiss Lake in the 1950s, will take the lead in helping to ensure that "our lake" will still be here in another fifty years.

ACKNOWLEDGEMENTS

Despite the sparse official record, the story of Cherokee County before, during and after the construction of Weiss Lake was safe and sound in the minds of the people who lived it. All I had to do to compile this collection was ask a few questions, listen to the answers and make sure I spelled the names correctly when I wrote them down. If I ever had any illusions that I would be able to compile a complete, comprehensive history of the construction of Weiss Lake and its effects on Cherokee County in one publication, I got a reality check pretty quickly. Everyone I talked with named at least one other person who had a story they were certain I would want to hear. For the most part, they were right every time.

As a result, I didn't write this book as much as it wrote itself—and there was still plenty left to write when I reached the end of my thirty-thousand-word limit. Stories of the water quality in Weiss Lake and the ever-intensifying fight with Georgia to receive a fair share of the Coosa River would each fill an entire book. I didn't even mention the fate of construction giant Morrison-Knudsen, but that is another story just waiting to be written. Practically every campground and boat launch has a unique history that I was unable to include this time around, and I never even mentioned Liberty Day, Cedar Bluff's annual ode to the tourist trade in Cherokee County. Hundreds of other people were every bit as instrumental as the Tuckers in rejuvenating the county's efforts to promote Weiss Lake. Unfortunately, space restrictions prevented me from mentioning more than a few. The list of shortcomings goes on and on, but I will hang onto every voice recording, every photocopy and every page of notes, and I ask anyone with a lake-related story to tell to contact me via email at swright@postpaper.com. Maybe we can combine what I have with what you're willing to share and further expand the documented history of Weiss Lake.

I am most grateful to my employers, David and Elizabeth Crawford, for allowing me to take time from my job as managing editor of *The Post* to work on this project. Without their patience and understanding, my book about a dam would have been a damned disaster. (Perhaps it is anyway; I will leave that judgment to the reader.) I am also extremely grateful to a trio of historians who have spent far more than their fair share of time in the "Way Back Machine": Alabama Power Company archivist Bill Tharpe, Jacksonville State University history department head Hardy Jackson and Alabama Power historian Leah Atkins. Between them, they have paddled up and down the Coosa River more times than any circa-1890 riverboat ever did. Their years of hard work collecting and communicating history made my task easy by comparison.

John Wilkinson and his coworkers at The History Press believed my proposal was a good idea, and I appreciate their faith in me and the importance they saw in telling a tiny piece of the history of Weiss Lake. Thanks for the leap of faith, Boss. As the reader knows by now, the copyeditors and design staff at The History Press did more than their fair share toward turning a pile of paragraphs and a few old photos into what I hope readers will consider to be a respectable effort.

The entire staff of the Cherokee County Public Library has my undying gratitude for their tireless efforts to find whatever tiny puzzle piece I needed to complete first sentences, then paragraphs, then chapters. Coworkers Kristin Chancellor Cambron and Tina Arnold handled dozens of phone messages, forwarded e-mails and picked up the slack at *The Post* on those crazy Friday mornings when I wasn't where I was supposed to be. Thanks, guys. My tenth-grade history teacher, Sarah Benefield, was the first to read an early draft of the manuscript, and I thank her for not laughing out loud. Kevyn Bowling, Sumer Gaymon-Buckner and *Cherokee County Herald* editor Kathy Roe picked up their red pens when I asked. I appreciate their considerable contributions to the final manuscript. I would tell my attorney, Shane Givens, to send me a bill for the assistance he provided, but I'm scared to death he would actually do it. In lieu of payment, my sincere gratitude will have to suffice.

I am also indebted to the following people for their time, photos, advice and memories, not to mention their patience with a first-time author who was mostly feeling his way: Bob and Louise Nelson; Forrest and Peggy Pearson; Doris Pearson; George and Julia Coheley; Kenny Gossett; Sarah Gossett Wright; Martha Sue Wright; Martha Baker; John and Leisa Boggs; Jerry Culberson; Bobby Joe Johnson; William Johnson; Billy Godfrey; Mike Ward; Sue Young; Ted Pyron; Leo Grady; Bert Latham; Gary and Vivian Mobbs;

Reverend Gary Hardin; Ralph and Nancy Meade; Bill Moss; Hack Sain; Curt Tucker; Jason Tucker; Carolyn Landrem; Shad Ellis; John Awbrey; Marshall Macomber; Tony O'Neal; Dean Buttram Jr.; Vicki Wright, my mom; Heather Blackmon; Barbara Cochran; Thereasa Hulgan; Scooter Howell; Tommy and Nell Oliver; and Jimmy Wallace. I apologize sincerely to the dozens of others I have completely forgotten. Thank you all for your help getting this book into print.

I didn't forget about you, Dad. Thanks for the memories. I will treasure them forever.

SELECTED BIBLIOGRAPHY

Atkins, Leah Rawls. *Developed for the Service of Alabama: The Centennial History of the Alabama Power Company, 1906–2006*. Birmingham: Alabama Power Co., 2006.

Cemeteries Impacted by Weiss Dam and Lake of Cherokee County, Alabama. Gadsden: privately published by the Northeast Alabama Genealogical Society, 2005.

Cherokee County, A Pictorial History 1836–1986. Centre, AL: privately published by the Sesquicentennial History Book Committee, 1986.

Coosa/Warrior Relicensing Project: Initial Information Packet for the Weiss Development. Springfield, VA: privately published by Kleinschmidt Energy and Water Resource Consultants for Alabama Power Co., 2000.

History and Heritage: Articles on Cherokee County, Alabama. Centre, AL: privately published by the Cherokee County Historical Museum, 1972.

Jackson, Harvey H., III. *Rivers of History: Life on the Coosa, Tallapoosa, Cahaba and Alabama*. Tuscaloosa: University of Alabama Press, 1995.

Weiss Lake Resource Management and Projection Plan. Anniston: privately published by the East Alabama Regional Planning and Development Commission for the Cherokee County Chamber of Commerce, 1997.

Weiss 2000 Initiative: Recommendations to the Cherokee County Commission and Cherokee County Board of Health. Centre, AL: privately published by the Cherokee County Chamber of Commerce, 1996.

Young, Roscoe. *REA Pioneer and Life Long Democrat.* Cherokee County, AL: privately published by Roscoe Young, circa 1975.